# FAITHFULNESS
# IN
# ACTION

# OVERTURES TO BIBLICAL THEOLOGY

A series of studies in biblical theology designed to explore fresh dimensions of research and to suggest ways in which the biblical heritage may address contemporary culture

*Editors*

WALTER BRUEGGEMANN, Professor of Old Testament at Eden Theological Seminary, St. Louis, Missouri

JOHN R. DONAHUE, S.J., Professor of New Testament at the Jesuit School of Theology, Berkeley, California

*Loyalty*
*in*
*Biblical*
*Perspective*

# FAITHFULNESS
# IN
# ACTION

KATHARINE DOOB SAKENFELD

FORTRESS PRESS      Philadelphia

---

**Library of Congress Cataloging in Publication Data**

Sakenfeld, Katharine Doob, 1940–
   Faithfulness in action.
   (Overtures to Biblical theology; 16)
   Includes index.
   1. Loyalty—Biblical teaching.  2. Bible—Theology.
I. Title.  II. Series.
BS680.L65S25  1985    220.6    84–18738
ISBN 0–8006–1540–9

---

1279G84   Printed in the United States of America  1–1540

To my parents
Hilda Smith Doob
Hugo Doob, jr.
whose lives overflow with
faithfulness in action

# Contents

# Editor's Foreword

In her first book, *The Meaning of Ḥesed in the Hebrew Bible* (Missoula, Mont.: Scholars Press, 1978), Katharine Doob Sakenfeld pursued fresh, basic research concerning Old Testament meanings of faithfulness. In the present volume she advances those studies in important ways, with keen theological sensitivity and with a discerning eye on contemporary, societal issues.

Three comments are in order by way of editorial presentation:

First, Sakenfeld's procedure is shrewdly and carefully chosen. She begins, not with theological premises, but with narratives of human mutuality and fidelity. That is, at the outset she eschews any grand theological theory and builds her understanding from concrete human experience. In this procedure, she is faithful to the Bible itself, which does theology "upward" from actual human experience. It follows then, that God's faithfulness is by way of analogy to or metaphor from human experience. To be sure, the claims made for God's faithfulness do not stop there and run well beyond human experience, which is always a scarred and inadequate fidelity.

Second, Sakenfeld dares to take on the vexed question of covenant. It has been too dogmatically claimed (and too dogmatically denied) that covenant is central to Israel's faith. There is little doubt that *ḥesed* has important connections to covenant. But Sakenfeld is not trapped by any of those scholarly fixations. She proceeds toward covenantal affirmation about God and Israel, not by way of a general hypothesis but by observation about specific moments of faithful relationship. She observes that such a commitment of loyalty on the part of God leads to hurt, anguish, and pathos on God's part. At the end, we arrive at a vigorous affirmation of covenant, but arrived at by a quite fresh route.

Third, in her beginning point and in her bold conclusion, the author pays attention to contemporary issues. Our social situation is one of ethical dogmatism about right and wrong, or conversely, a self-serving individualism which sustains and values no enduring commitments. In such a context, Israel's understanding of faithfulness both with neighbor and with God is a powerful and distinctive resource. In this literature lies the promise of and offer of a fidelity that not only refuses rigidity but also equally rejects isolation.

Readers of this book will find Sakenfeld helpful and resonant on two important issues in our contemporary situation. First, it is clear that there is a fresh search for persons in our culture concerning serious interpersonal commitment. The vogue of self-actualization has run its course and has ended, predictably, in isolation and loneliness. Sakenfeld's exposition of the theme of *ḥesed* shows ways in which serious, enduring, and life-giving interpersonal loyalty was produced in ancient Israel, which may indeed be a suggestive model in our own situation.

Second, there is a yearning in our time for the presence of a God who is personally available and concerned for individual persons. This study makes clear that the only two alternatives are *not* a public God who deals only with the rise and fall of nations on the one hand and a mushy romanticism on the other hand. The God who produces *ḥesed* is indeed concerned for individual persons, but in ways that have character, seriousness, and quality. Both in the love of *God's availability* and *human interpersonal commitment,* Sakenfeld shows the way in which biblical faith offers discernment and resources for our own cultural situation. Her understanding of *ḥesed* makes an important companion for the notion of "friend" so ably sketched out by Sallie McFague in *Metaphorical Theology* (Philadelphia: Fortress Press, 1982).

The broad outlines of God's faithfulness have, of course, been well-known. But this re-reading lets us see much that we have missed. Sakenfeld thus raises important questions, not only about exegetical substance but also about the interpretive process. The two belong together. The combination here is a welcome articulation.

WALTER BRUEGGEMANN

# Preface

Let not loyalty and faithfulness forsake you;
  bind them about your neck,
  write them on the tablet of your heart.
                                                 (Prov. 3:3)

This study of biblical perspectives on loyalty presents a significant expansion of selected theological themes from my earlier
work, *The Meaning of Ḥesed in the Hebrew Bible* (Missoula,
Mont.: Scholars Press, 1978). Much of the technical work of that
volume is presupposed, but this volume stands on its own as an
"overture."

Bible quotations follow the Revised Standard Version unless
otherwise identified (i.e., au. trans.), except that I have consistently substituted "loyalty" for the various RSV translations of
Hebrew *ḥesed*. "Sure loyalty" is sometimes substituted for the
RSV renderings of *ḥesed we'ĕmet*. Verse numbers are given according to the English text.

I express my appreciation to Princeton Theological Seminary for
a sabbatical in which to think and write, and to the Association of
Theological Schools for a grant which helped to support my research and writing. Thanks are due also to Walter Brueggemann
for his support and suggestions as series editor. Typists Elizabeth
Mcirs and Eugenia Bishop have worked cheerfully and beyond the
call of duty.

I am especially grateful to my colleagues Bernhard Anderson
and Freda Gardner for long hours of conversation and for

painstaking reading of portions of the manuscript. Their helpful suggestions have done much to improve the final result.

The loyalty which my husband Helmar extended during the writing of the manuscript only continued the wonderful faithfulness he has shown me over the years. The volume is dedicated with honor and affection to my parents, who know what it means to write loyalty and faithfulness on the tablets of their hearts.

KATHARINE DOOB SAKENFELD
Princeton, New Jersey
September, 1983

# Abbreviations

| | |
|---|---|
| AB | Anchor Bible |
| ATANT | Abhandlungen zur Theologie des Alten und Neuen Testaments |
| *BASOR* | *Bulletin of the American Schools of Oriental Research* |
| *BZAW* | Beihefte zur *Zeitschrift für die alttestamentliche Wissenschaft* |
| *CBQ* | *Catholic Biblical Quarterly* |
| HSM | Harvard Semitic Monographs |
| *IDB* | *Interpreter's Dictionary of the Bible* |
| IDBSup | Supplementary volume to *IDB* |
| *JBL* | *Journal of Biblical Literature* |
| JSOTSup | *Journal for the Study of Old Testament,* Supplement Series |
| NAB | New American Bible |
| OTL | Old Testament Library |
| RSV | Revised Standard Version |
| *VT* | *Vetus Testamentum* |
| VTSup | *Vetus Testamentum,* Supplements |

CHAPTER 1

# Introduction:
# Contemporary Experience
# and Ancient Witness

A husband and wife are contemplating divorce. Their marriage counselor urges each in turn to consider self-fulfillment as the primary criterion in reaching a decision. . . . A young woman discovers that getting ahead in her business means loyalty to her corporate employer, loyalty which goes beyond long hours and on into the murky area of tampering with research results. . . . A teenager in Los Angeles (or New York or Chicago) discovers that the only way of survival is to join one of the competing gangs of his neighborhood. . . . Everywhere people complain that they are only cogs in some unnamed machine (work, government, society in general), and they search for some kind of commitment that can give meaning and structure to their lives. The old standbys of family, work, and neighborhood are not what they used to be—or at least not what we nostalgically remember them to be. We flip-flop from setting to setting, from day to day, between living as loners, loyal only to ourselves, and living as co-opted beings, tied to whatever relationship beyond self holds out some hope of meaning.

The scenario is discouragingly somber, but not unrealistic. In an age when small children have nightmares of nuclear holocaust and many college students expect that atomic warfare will snuff out their lives prematurely, words like "faithfulness" and "loyalty" have lost their power. It is increasingly difficult to think of long-term commitments. The question "What's in it for me?" tends to take priority over the question "How can I be useful?"—if only

1

because being useful and being used are so difficult for us to distinguish. We struggle with the tension between our own rights and our duties toward the rights of others.[1] In such a world, it is hard to know how to appropriate the biblical exhortation:

> Let not loyalty and faithfulness forsake you;
>    bind them about your neck,
>    write them on the tablet of your heart.
>                               (Prov. 3:3)

While it is true that we experience the difficulties of faithful and loyal living in peculiar ways in our own time and culture, the same kinds of questions have been faced by people in every generation. Biblical people, those whose biographies are recorded in the Bible, those whose prophecies, songs, histories, reflections, or letters are handed on to us, faced the questions of faithfulness and loyalty as well. The chapters that follow examine the resources of the Old Testament heritage for addressing this ancient yet contemporary problem.

This study focuses particularly on texts and traditions in which the Hebrew term *hesed* appears. The word itself is notoriously difficult to translate; commentaries and handbooks regularly mention the complexity of the term. Its rendering was one of the last decisions worked through by the first-edition Revised Standard Version translators.[2] A recent monograph by Edgar Kellenberger reviews at its conclusion no fewer than a dozen German translation options and indicates the inadequacy of any one possibility taken alone.[3] The English word "loyalty," which will be used predominantly in this volume, has its own shortcomings as a translation equivalent. Some of these should be noted in particular. First, English usage sometimes equates loyalty with the quite negative concept of blind obedience, which we will find is not part of the biblical picture. Second, the word "loyalty" is often used in English for the attitude that a subordinate should exhibit toward a superior, but rarely the other way round. We will discover that the biblical notion of *hesed*/loyalty refers more often to just the opposite direction of relationship: the powerful is loyal to the weak or needy or dependent. Finally, in English usage loyalty tends to be conceived of as an attitude. That attitude needs to be tested by action, but then we must refer to "acts of loyalty" or "demonstrations of loyalty." In Hebrew, by contrast, the word *ḥesed* encompasses both the attitude and the action. The Hebrew noun *ḥesed* is often the object of the verb "to do," and keeps its action-connotation even when such a verb is not present. With these caveats in mind, the reader is invited to break open the horizons of the English term "loyalty" as we explore its rich biblical sense of "faithfulness in action."

Any biblical theological inquiry into the meaning of faithful relationship might well begin by a consideration of God's ways of relating to humanity. Surely the Old Testament writers witness again and again to the divine initiative—with the whole human race in Adam and Eve or Noah, with the people of God in Abraham and Sarah or Moses or David. The life style expected of the holy community and the life styles expected of individuals within that community ought to reflect God's ways with the people. The theme is epitomized in the words of Lev. 19:2:

> Say to all the congregation of the people of Israel, You shall be holy; for I the Lord your God am holy.

Micah's call for Israel's loyalty (Mic. 6:8) is properly viewed as consequent upon God's loyalty to the community. Despite the theological centrality of the order God–Israel–individual in the larger perspective of the Old Testament, this volume begins by exploring some stories of loyalty between individuals in ancient Israel. Three important and interconnected considerations lie behind this choice of a beginning point.

First, it should be recognized that whenever we speak of the loyalty or faithfulness of God, we are speaking anthropomorphically. While we notice this anthropomorphic element readily enough when we speak of the face or hand of God, we tend to overlook it when we turn to highly charged theological terms such as "faithful" or "righteous." Somehow it seems as if we know the content of these terms, and that such understanding frees them from their anthropomorphic character. But when we are called upon to explain the meaning of such words, to describe their content, the illustrations that we give relate to modes of behavior rooted in human experience. We say, for instance, that the God of the Bible, conceived of personally, is the One who cares for the poor, who brings down the kingdoms of wicked rulers, who never abandons the faithful. To determine what phrases may best infuse content into Israel's conception of God's loyalty, we need therefore to examine the Old Testament record, to discover what anthropomorphic word pictures the ancient writers themselves have chosen to give expression to this aspect of God's relationship to their community. We need to discover ancient Israel's own frame of reference.

This recognition of the ambiguity of anthropomorphic language leads to a second consideration. In looking for biblical expressions describing God's loyalty, one finds that such concrete images are few and far between in texts that speak directly of divine faithfulness to Israel. The passages about God's loyalty are concentrated in the psalms, where the singer praises that loyalty or prays that it be made manifest. There the content of the vocabulary is usually assumed rather than given concrete illustration, so that one must look elsewhere for clues as to the meaning of loyalty.

The references to the term in narrative contexts can provide such needed clues. When the word appears as part of a story, the narrative itself offers some indicators of the meaning of loyalty for the biblical authors. The Bible includes both narratives with references to divine loyalty (usually to individuals) and also those with references to the loyalty of individuals to one another. Of these two types of story, the latter are more numerous; also, the detail is usually greater in the case of these narratives about human interrelationships. Such texts about human loyalty thus provide a helpful starting point for this study, on two grounds: they serve as a reminder of the anthropomorphic character of biblical God-talk, and they provide possible pointers to the nuances of such vocabulary. As the study moves on to examine theological dimensions of loyalty, it can explore the pressures that come upon this anthropomorphic language because the Holy One is "divine, not human" (Hos. 11:9); it can note ways in which the theological usage is modified to try to overcome the inadequacy of the an-thropomorphic usage.[4]

A third consideration also suggests that this study begin with a focus on narratives about interpersonal relationships. Here I have in mind the various modern conceptions of loyalty mentioned above. If we hope that the Bible will address us and our own generation in a lively way, part of our effort to improve our hearing ability must consist in developing a certain self-awareness. We need to lift our own notions of loyalty to a more self-conscious level of reflection. Such reflection may be readily opened up by considering our own ways of identifying demonstrations or failures of loyalty in the light of loyalty lived out by biblical characters as portrayed in narrative. We have, I believe, a greater likelihood of hearing a biblical word about God's loyalty to us if we move toward it (or let it move toward us) by the indirect route of testing facets of the Hebrew view of human loyalty against aspects of our own concepts of loyalty. The goal is, of course, much more than to compare our personal biographies with those of Israelite women and men. We are seeking insight into an attitude, a way of living out relationships with others, in which God's loyalty, not David's or Sarah's or Ahab's, is the ultimate model and criterion. The ancient biographies serve as a step along the way, as a springboard for understanding more clearly some biblical perspectives on God's relationship to us.

For these reasons, then, the following discussion begins by ex-ploring some narrative clues to the Old Testament conception of loyalty between persons. This material will open the way for con-sidering the character of God's loyalty to Israel and to individual members of the household of faith. Divine loyalty in turn provides the backdrop for examining the Old Testament view of communal and individual loyalty to God as response to God's initiative. Some reflection on contemporary implications of this biblical perspective on loyalty conclude the study.

## NOTES

1. Daniel Yankelovitch (*New Rules: Searching for Self-Fulfillment in a World Turned Upside Down* [New York: Random House, 1981]) has

described the emergence of this tension among modern Americans as a movement from an inadequate ethic of self-denial to a flawed search for self-fulfillment focused on material acquisition and/or on a "me first" outlook on life. His case interviews graphically testify to his respondents' confusion about the place of loyalty or commitment in their lives.

2. Their decision was to use "steadfast love" consistently for God's *ḥesed*; for human *ḥesed*, various terms are used, predominantly "kindness" and occasionally "loyalty."

3. Edgar Kellenberger, *ḥäsäd wä'ämät als Ausdruck einer Glaubenserfahrung*, ATANT 69 (Zurich: Theologischer Verlag, 1982).

4. Sallie McFague underlines the importance of this effort to step back from and examine the supposedly self-evident meaning of language in the first chapter of her *Metaphorical Theology: Models of God in Religious Language* (Philadelphia: Fortress Press, 1982). McFague emphasizes that the basic mode of human thinking is metaphorical; hence metaphorical thinking is involved in theological concepts and models as well as in images for God (such as king or father or friend). "Concepts and theories, however, . . . rarely expose their metaphorical roots" (p. 26). Whether divine loyalty is viewed as a concept, or whether "the Loyal One" is treated as a metaphor for God, the challenge is to identify the particular dimensions of this language which were first of all specific to the biblical writers.

CHAPTER 2

# Stories

# of Human Loyalty

The biblical narratives that speak explicitly of loyalty in human interaction are clustered in Genesis, Ruth, and the corpus of the Deuteronomic history (Deuteronomy—2 Kings). These stories of loyalty are greatly varied: the acts of loyalty undertaken range from lying to spying, from marrying to burying, from providing food to granting life. The people involved range from an Israelite king to a desperate widow, from familiar heroes to folk who are never otherwise mentioned. The risk involved in acting loyally may be great or small, so long as one person's genuine need for loyalty from the other is clear.

The stories divide themselves readily into the two main kinds of relationships in which people of our own time also participate: relationships that involve family members and relationships that are basically public in character. This second group would be typified today by relationships on the job scene or in community projects. In the biblical narratives, examples of this nonfamily type of relationship are centered mainly in the arenas of politics and warfare, simply because much of the Old Testament narrative concentrates on recording national history, where such topics are prominent. Modern people often recognize a third category of relationship, that of a close personal friend who is nevertheless not a blood relation; this "intermediate" category too appears in the biblical narrative.

In this chapter we begin with stories of King David. The most familiar of these stories—involving Jonathan—combines the close

friend and the political spheres of relationship. The other David
stories are predominantly political. The chapter continues with
a sampling of other stories from the political sphere and concludes with an exploration of several narratives about family
relationships.

STORIES OF DAVID

The narrative of David's arrival at the household of King Saul,
Jonathan's father, and of his relationship with Saul (1 Samuel 16—
2 Samuel 5) reflects a complex history of tradition. Popular folk
memories are collected and strung together, so that one frequently
has the sense that the story line is repeating itself or giving an
alternate version of a remembered event. Commentators have
often sought to sort out these materials by grouping them into two
or more internally consistent "sources." More helpful is the recent
analysis by P. Kyle McCarter, Jr.: An old source concerning "the
history of David's rise" was brought together by a "prophetic
writer" with two other sources concerning the ark of the covenant
and the early career of Saul (1 Samuel 1—15). This compiler
viewed kingship as a divine concession to a weak and sinful people
but wanted also to suggest guidelines for how this negatively
viewed kingship ought to operate in Israel; he revised and supplemented his old sources to emphasize these concerns. In a final
stage, supplementation was added by the Deuteronomic historian.[1] Many of the tensions in the narrative result from layers of
reworking, while others represent divergent old traditions left
intact by those who first gathered them.

A second large complex of David material is found in the so-
called "court history" or "succession narrative" (2 Samuel 9—
1 Kings 2). This narrative unit covers his career from the death of
Saul and Jonathan until David's own death. Additional shorter
units have been incorporated in the transmission and redaction of
the history of Israel's best-remembered king.

*David and Jonathan*

Of the many loyal relationships depicted in Old Testament narrative, that of David and Jonathan is perhaps the most familiar.

The paired names epitomize faithful relationship in the minds of many modern people, even though the details of the story of these two famous men may be vague or unfamiliar. Theirs is a story of the tensions between personal friendship and political realities.

Despite unevenness in the details of the narrative, the basic contours of the relationships linking David, Saul, and Jonathan are clear. Saul is at first apparently delighted by David but later sees David as a threat and seeks in many ways to take David's life. The tradition is interested in preserving a long sequence of the incidents of Saul against David, both because they make good adventure narrative and because their consistent outcome shows David's cleverness, his protection by God, and his respect for the office of kingship even in the villain Saul. Even though David has already been anointed as future king by Samuel before he first meets Saul, according to the final form of the tradition (1 Samuel 16—17), David is not willing to hasten Saul's demise in order to protect himself or to pursue his own advantage. It is only against this backdrop that we can properly appreciate the relationship between David and Jonathan and particularly the situation of Jonathan.

The institution of kingship is at this point in its infancy, so much so that the term "institution" should probably be used only in retrospect. The biblical narrative itself refers often to Saul and even to David as *nāgîd* (traditionally translated "prince" but more accurately understood as a warrior-leader) rather than exclusively as *melek* ("king"). Certainly it was not self-evident what principle of succession would be invoked as the kingship of Saul was passed on to his successor. The theological issue at the heart of the David story is this question of succession; the narrative plot centers on it. Should the throne go to Jonathan as Saul's son? The narrative indicates that Saul presumed Jonathan should inherit the kingship (1 Sam. 20:31), and the old source concerning David's rise (1 Samuel 16—2 Samuel 5) recounts Saul's many efforts to quash David. The "prophetic" editor's prefixing of God's rejection of Saul and choice of David (1 Sam. 15:1—16:13) to the story of David's rise serves indirectly to highlight Saul's viewpoint by making him seem more determined than ever that he and his should retain rule. At the same time, this prefixed material encapsulates an alternative approach to simple hereditary succession: succession will be decided by the word of the prophet rather than by bloodline alone. In the long view, we are told that Israel and Judah functioned under a combination of these two principles. David's irrevocable blood dynasty was announced by the prophet Nathan. The dynastic history of north Israel in 1 and 2 Kings shows that the bloodline principle was operative there as well, but prophetic announcement of God's new choice is presented as functioning in at least some changes in dynasty.

This complexity of the historical transition to kingship, compounded by the complexity of the traditions about the transition, results in a story of the relationship between David and Jonathan which is likewise complex and multifaceted. David the harpist and giant slayer is befriended by Jonathan the potential crown prince (1 Samuel 18); Jonathan seeks to dissuade his father from killing David and wins a temporary respite (1 Samuel 19); Jonathan covers for David's absence and thus enrages Saul, who then even tries to kill Jonathan (1 Samuel 20); Jonathan admits David's future place as king (1 Samuel 23), but returns home and dies beside his father, Saul, in battle (1 Samuel 31). All of the interaction between Jonathan and David involves both personal and political dimensions; given their roles, it is impossible for political realities to be ignored, and yet the relationship is rooted in something deeper than expediency for either participant. What does loyalty look like in their lives?

The first explicit references to loyalty come in 1 Samuel 20 (vv. 8, 14, 15), sometime after Jonathan has established a covenant with David (18:3). The basic material of the chapter comes from the old history of David's rise, but vv. 11–17 appear to be an interpolation by the hand that joined this material to the story of David's rule in 2 Samuel.[2] According to the basic narrative of 1 Samuel 20, Jonathan knows nothing of Saul's plotting against David. In the received tradition this plot must be viewed as a new attempt by Saul, since Jonathan has already saved David by temporarily dissuading Saul from his murderous intent (1 Samuel 19). Now Jonathan offers David his help (20:4) and David outlines a plan for testing Saul's intentions (vv. 5–7). He concludes by urging

Jonathan to show loyalty to him (RSV "deal kindly"), because of the covenant relationship which Jonathan has initiated between the two men. Several features of this situation in which David pleads for loyalty are important for an understanding of biblical loyalty.

First of all, this occasion involves a matter of life and death for David. Loyalty is not invoked over some trivial affair, but over a situation of utmost seriousness. David genuinely needs Jonathan's help. Even though Jonathan is not yet fully convinced of the danger to David, his act of loyalty will begin by taking David seriously enough that he investigates the situation.[3]

The call to loyalty here is also a call to Jonathan to choose an attitude toward David in a situation of conflict. "If there is guilt in me, slay me yourself," says David, "for why should you bring me to your father?" (v. 8). Jonathan is challenged to affirm David's right to live in the face of the covenant between them. It is worth noting that the expression of loyalty is put in terms of a choice for David's life, not as a choice between David and Saul. Although Jonathan's struggle is not developed by the biblical narrator, the reader can scarcely miss the possibility that loyalty to Jonathan's friend, David, suggests disloyalty to his father, Saul; the bond of covenant and the bond of blood relationship here impose conflicting demands. Jonathan chooses for David and covenant, and his choice forms an important part of the narrator's case for the legitimacy of David's kingship. The narrator wants to emphasize that even Jonathan, an heir apparent, took David's part. Yet, as has been said, the text never presents Jonathan's choice as being explicitly against his father, Saul. Saul perceives Jonathan's behavior as against his own father when he castigates his son with the words "Do I not know that you have chosen the son of Jesse to your own shame, and to the shame of your mother's nakedness?" (v. 30). The enraged father then vents his fury by throwing his spear at Jonathan for insisting upon David's innocence. But Jonathan's anger and grief at his father's response (v. 34) emphasize his own refusal to view his loyalty to David as rejection of his father. He never separates himself from his father; David's lament over their deaths puts the point simply: "In life and in death they were not divided" (2 Sam. 1:23).

In this instance the loyalty that David asks of Jonathan is based in a "covenant" *(bĕrît)* relationship. The situation is not merely one between friends, although we are surely to understand a deep friendship between the two. Rather, there is a formally established pact, initiated by Jonathan (1 Sam. 18:1–4). The statement connected with the establishing of this pact, that Jonathan "loved David as himself," is probably to be understood not simply as personal affection or attraction but also as having political overtones[4] and thus as a foreshadowing of Jonathan's eventual recognition of David as the future king. The gifts of robe, armor, and weapons may anticipate that recognition as well. In David's plea for loyalty, he not only reminds Jonathan of their formal relationship; he also declares that there has been no breach on his part, when he adds, "If there is guilt in me, slay me yourself." In biblical usage it is important in requesting an act of loyalty to establish the quality of the relationship between the two people involved. The covenant allusion reminds Jonathan of his moral responsibility to accede to David's plea.

The complexity of the relationship and circumstances here precludes any labeling of who is the superior and who is the subordinate in this instance. The two men are friends and in this respect on equal footing. Yet Jonathan is the king's son and initiator of the covenant, while David is only a court member on the run. On the other hand, David is the one designated by God as future king, and Jonathan's covenant may anticipate David in that role. So a specific structure of authority is not attached to the concept of loyalty here. At the same time, it is obvious that at this particular juncture David is "situationally inferior" because his life is apparently in danger; he must appeal to Jonathan for help in assessing Saul's attitude and deciding on his next move. In the situation as the narrator presents it, Jonathan is uniquely able to assist David in this moment of need, for Jonathan is the one person at the king's table with whom David has a close personal tie. And Jonathan agrees not only to assess Saul's attitude but also personally to let David know how matters stand and what he should do.

To summarize: Loyalty in this brief narrative involves a serious need on the part of the recipient (here life itself); loyalty is not a matter of doing some casual favor which really would not affect the quality and structure of the relationship. Loyalty is called for in a context of potential conflict, but the conflict is implicit and the one who shows loyalty is not said to have chosen directly against someone else. Loyalty comes into play in the context of an existing relationship; it is an act which strengthens the relationship, but not one which first brings the relationship into being.[5] In this instance the relationship is one formally established between the parties, and one noted by the person in need to be in good repair, not damaged by any wrongdoing on his part. The act of loyalty requested is not tied to any social pattern of superior/subordinate within the relationship; the only "ranking" is in the matter of need, where one is in dire straits and the other is especially able to respond to the need by a particular action. All of these factors taken together suggest that the act of loyalty here is an act of moral, but not formally legal, responsibility. Because of the circumstances, the moral decision is also one that can be privately made. If Jonathan fails to carry through, no one will be the wiser, except David—who will possibly be dead but in any case will be in no position to bring any reprisal against Jonathan. The relationship will in effect be ended if Jonathan does not act. Jonathan is bound from a moral point of view, yet he is free from a practical point of view. The action requested of him may harm him in the short run or help him in the long run. He cannot know for certain; but the call to loyal action commensurate with his relationship to David is clear, and Jonathan accepts it. In reviewing other narratives of loyal action, we will see that variations on these basic characteristics appear again and again.

The encounter between David and Jonathan continues with Jonathan's oath to reveal Saul's attitude to David and then Jonathan's request that David exercise loyalty toward him and his household. This request (1 Sam. 20:14–17) anticipates David's action toward Jonathan's son Meribaal (Mephibosheth) in 2 Samuel 9, and the two parts of the story may be considered together. Although the Hebrew text of 1 Sam. 20:14–15 is difficult and all of

vv. 12–17 bristles with textual problems,[6] the general thrust of Jonathan's request for loyalty can be discerned. No specific action is proposed, but the relationship is to be maintained not only between the two men themselves but also, after Jonathan's death, between David and the surviving household of Jonathan. David eventually carries out this commitment by specifically seeking out and befriending Jonathan's son Meribaal (Mephibosheth).

In the process of David's being established as king, his principal opposition apparently lay in Ishbosheth, another son of Saul, and in Abner, Saul's general. Both these men were killed by supporters of David (2 Samuel 3—4), and David is reported to have been angered in each instance. David's attitude can be interpreted as a genuine desire to gain power through diplomacy and consent, or more crassly as a way to gain more favor from events that he secretly appreciated and that (the most cynical might suggest) he might even have helped to plan. The same speculation about actual motives attaches itself to the befriending of Meribaal, a crippled young man (2 Sam. 4:1–4) living in a part of Transjordan that may have been a stronghold for renegade Saulides. David initiates, for the sake of Jonathan, a search for a survivor of the household of Saul. He has Jonathan's son Meribaal brought to a place at the royal table, "like one of the king's sons." Thus the name of Jonathan is not cut off from the household of David. And by indirection the narrator indicates also that David's respect for Saul as the Lord's anointed remained undiminished, for even in this narrative the household of Saul (not simply the person of Jonathan) is in the foreground; in death as in life, Saul and Jonathan are not divided.

It is not by chance that Jonathan first declares his commitment to help David before making his own request for loyalty. Although Jonathan's request follows immediately, there is no directly stated condition (such as, "I will do this if you promise me . . ."), nor even an explicit connection (such as, "Because I will do this, you should promise . . ."). The commitment of both partners to the relationship is the sufficient basis for action now and for expectation of future loyalty.[7] David acts "for the sake of . . . Jonathan" (2 Sam. 9:7), not because Jonathan did such and such for David. The acts give life to the relationship, but they are not measured tit for tat on some quantified contractual basis.

Here in Jonathan's request, as in David's, a matter of great seriousness is at stake. Jonathan may need protection at once if his father is angered by his support of David. But the author has an even longer perspective in view, as we see in the expression "When the Lord cuts off every one of the enemies of David from the face of the earth" (1 Sam. 20:15), which anticipates David's final establishment as king. When the roles of the two households are reversed, when David rules and the Saulides are in flight and hiding, then the pact is remembered and honored. David's action for Meribaal is a matter of good life and security versus exile and fear. Living loyally means honoring relationships over time and in drastic change of circumstance. In the relationship between king and subject, it is here the king who is showing loyalty; the emphasis, however, is not upon their particular social roles as superior or subordinate, but upon the household relationship and the opportunity of the man with power to act loyally toward the man in need.

Like Jonathan before him, David acts in a situation of moral demand but practical freedom of decision. It takes positive initiative on his part to locate Meribaal and summon him to Jerusalem. Certainly David could have ignored Jonathan's son and done something else with Saul's land. It is not possible to say absolutely which course of action would have been more convenient; but the tradition ties David's decision to his commitment to Jonathan, not to expediency. A tradition that does not shrink from showing us David's faults (notably in respect to Bathsheba and Uriah) wants also to show us a man who understood the meaning of loyal living.

David's exercise of loyalty to Meribaal of the household of Jonathan is the opening scene in the "court history" of David, or "succession narrative," mentioned above. This narrative reviews life at David's court and describes the competition among his sons for the opportunity to succeed him. The author, conceivably an eyewitness or at least one close to the scene, mentions three other instances of loyalty that supplement the picture of loyalty between Jonathan and David which has emerged so far. These involve

Hanun, king of Ammon, Barzillai the Gileadite, and David's court adviser, Hushai.

### David and Hanun

The story which follows the installation of Meribaal in Jerusalem concerns David's relationship with the kingdom of Ammon in Transjordan after the death of its king Nahash. David proposes to "deal loyally with Hanun the son of Nahash, as his father dealt loyally with me" (2 Sam. 10:2; cf. 1 Chron. 19:1–2). The story ends with enmity and battle because Hanun's advisers persuade him that David's emissaries are actually spies to be sent home in humiliation. But David's stated intention is in many ways similar to his dealing with Saul's household for the sake of Jonathan. We know nothing of the former history of David and Nahash, but clearly David wishes to continue a faithful relationship into the next generation. The context here is one of international diplomacy, without the overtones of close personal friendship which are the undercurrent of the Jonathan story; by sending official condolences, David indicates his support of Hanun's rule over Ammon. The fear of the Ammonite advisers offers the clue to David's "nonloyal" alternative, namely, a quick attempt to take over the Ammonite territory in its time of potential instability. In view of David's expansion into Edom, Moab, and Philistia (2 Samuel 8), the Ammonites' fear was scarcely an idle one.[8]

A historian might speculate about David's actual intent in sending emissaries, but the biblical narrator describes it as an act of loyalty; for purposes of interpreting the concept of loyalty, it is appropriate to take the statement of David's intent at face value. This incident suggests that acting loyally involves refraining from misuse of an opportunity for domination. The narrative also implies that "dealing loyally" involves general behavior which reflects a basic attitude; David's loyalty was manifest in the particular act of sending representatives, but that one act scarcely exhausted the loyalty David intended.

The story of David and Hanun is important also because it shows us another characteristic of human loyalty as the Bible uses the word. Loyalty may be short-lived. The survival of loyalty between

people is heavily dependent upon its mutuality. Loyalty unac-
cepted or unappreciated is usually loyalty lost. The Ammonites'
humiliation of David's envoys results in military conflict and the
subjugation of Syria as well as Ammon to David's rule. The story is
in its own way so modern that contemporary analogies scarcely
need be mentioned. Expulsion of embassy officials for alleged
spying is not infrequent. Recall of ambassadors or refusal to receive official envoys is equally part of our own diplomatic scene.
The risk of escalation inheres in each incident; fear or a need to
save face sometimes seems to outweigh a reasoned approach. The
biblical narrator, of course, is mainly interested in reporting the
battle between Israel and Ammon-Syria. The background is therefore given very briefly, explaining only why the battle took place
(the enemy's fault). No value judgment (whether negative or
positive) is placed upon David's about-face. The word "fickle" is
probably too strong to be attached by modern hindsight to David's
loyalty to Hanun, since "fickle" usually implies change without
substantive reason. Was David's attitude toward Hanun unjustifi-
ably ephemeral? The many political details that entered into
David's decision are not known. From the narrator's viewpoint,
David was no doubt to be commended for attempting a relationship with Ammon rather than rushing ahead at once toward a
takeover. But in this incident we find a characteristic much in
common with contemporary experience in exercising faithfulness.
Loyalty in theory means standing by faithfully no matter what. But
in actual daily living, whether in international treaty contexts or in
marriages or friendships, the first breach by the other party brings
us quickly to the question of why we should bother to keep on. Our
feelings of loyalty, our attitudes toward the other, are very change-
able, very dependent upon the faithfulness of the other. Our
experience and David's are much the same.

### David and Barzillai

Yet a third allusion to loyalty carried across to the next generation is found in David's deathbed instructions to his son Solomon
(1 Kings 2). Here David speaks specifically of the fate of three
men. Two are to die, but Solomon is to "deal loyally" with the sons

of Barzillai the Gileadite and allow them to "eat at . . . table" with him (v. 7). The loyalty of Barzillai's family to David during his flight from Absalom (2 Sam. 19:31–39) is recalled as the basis for David's instruction. While the actions of Joab (who brought blood-guilt upon David) and Shimei (who cursed David) are not explicitly described as disloyalty, the context suggests the contrast. In this instance, as also in the stories concerning Meribaal and Hanun, a past relationship is continued to the offspring, and here is to be carried forward by the second generation on David's side as well.

The occasion on which Barzillai showed loyalty to David has many features in common with the Jonathan and Hanun stories. Absalom, who had been permitted to return to Jerusalem after a period of exile,[9] "stole the hearts of the Israelites" (2 Sam. 15:6) and then had himself proclaimed king in Hebron (v. 10). The circumstances forced David and his entourage to flee Jerusalem, lest Absalom kill the leadership and succeed in taking over the kingdom. Once again David is seen in a situation of desperate need; food and supplies are brought by Barzillai (2 Sam. 17:27–29) and two other men from Transjordan. From what little is recorded of this event, no special reason emerges to explain why Barzillai, an elderly and wealthy man (2 Sam. 19:32), should have taken this action to assist David, rather than remaining neutral to see the outcome of the power struggle. By his action Barzillai declared his position; he attached no stipulations to his aid. The text does not tell us whether there was a formal relationship between the two men beforehand, beyond that of king and subject. The important point is that Barzillai's situation left him quite free in his decision to help David. He may have had a moral obligation to the Lord's anointed, but the circumstances were such that there would have been no legal action against Barzillai and no loss of community standing if he had done nothing. He offered his assistance freely. And so King David, as he dies, wants to ensure the continuation of his own offering of loyalty which had already begun as Chimham (presumably Barzillai's son) joined the royal entourage (2 Sam. 19:38).

## Hushai and David

One other individual besides Barzillai is especially remembered as dealing loyally with David during Absalom's revolt. A man named Hushai, described as "David's friend,"[10] approaches Absalom and offers to join his cause (2 Sam. 16:15—17:16). Hushai actually makes this approach at David's request in order to serve as a spy in Absalom's camp (15:32–37). Absalom responds suspiciously/incredulously/sarcastically to Hushai's greeting, "Long live the king!" He asks, "Is this your loyalty to your friend [David]? Why did you not go with your friend?" (16:17). Here the narrator's literary artistry is at its best. The tone of Absalom's questions is clearly judgmental; Absalom implies that by abandoning David, Hushai has failed to act loyally. The truth, which the reader knows, is just the opposite, of course. The true but unspoken answer to Absalom's question is really, "Yes, this is my loyalty to David; I did not go with him, because he asked me to come to you." In his conspiracy Hushai answers instead with a declaration of his willingness to serve Absalom (v. 19). But the narrator prefaces Hushai's explicit (false) declaration of allegiance with a brilliantly ambiguous one which Absalom takes to refer to himself but which the reader can interpret to refer secretly to David: "For whom the Lord and this people and all the Israelites have chosen, his I will be, and with him I will remain" (v. 18). As the suspenseful story proceeds, Hushai manages to persuade Absalom to follow his advice, and also smuggles out word to David concerning Absalom's plans. Armed with this knowledge, David's forces defeat the insurgents.

Oddly enough, we hear nothing more of Hushai. One may imagine that his treachery was discovered and that he was killed for it; but that is only speculation. The word "treachery," of course, applies only to Hushai's relationship to Absalom, and to Absalom's point of view. For David and from the narrator's viewpoint, Hushai's was an act of loyalty. In this event we see again that loyalty is a quality to be demonstrated in a situation of urgent need. Although David as king is formally superior to his adviser, his life is now very much in Hushai's hands. In the context of their relationship, Hushai is called upon to take great risk. His acts of perjury, suggesting, information gathering, and reporting are in some degree parallel to those earlier ones of Jonathan in Saul's court. Both were seeking to thwart plans against David without necessarily having the demise of the antagonist as part of their intention. Neither could exercise loyalty by remaining on the sidelines. Despite these parallels, however, the nuances are different. Jonathan's situation lifts up the poignancy of dual commitment. Hushai's highlights risk and the need for hard choices in the exercise of loyalty. Here there seems to be no room for compromise. Choice for David must be against Absalom, even if his death is not intended.

The narrator presents the success of Hushai's ploy as the accomplishment of God's plan (17:14; cf. 15:31), and this notice, as well as the general story line, suggests the critical nature of Hushai's contribution to David's survival. The circumstances gave Hushai freedom of choice; his action on behalf of David was morally appropriate to their relationship, yet it could in no way be compelled. One might say that David "deserved" Hushai's loyalty because of their relationship, or that Hushai "owed" it to David; yet given David's uncertain future and the risk of the action, one would want also to say that Hushai's decision was a "gift" freely offered. Both of these dimensions must be affirmed in order to grasp the full scope of the biblical conception of loyalty. Obligation and free choice are held together.

The narratives that have been explored thus far provide a reasonably coherent picture of what loyalty entailed in the world of politics and public friendship within the political sphere. In each instance one person decides freely to maintain a relationship with another individual or group. As might be expected in a narrative situation, the issue of loyalty arises when circumstances offer the possibility of a conflicting loyalty at the recipient's expense. Such conflict may involve another person or group, or it may be simply a matter of considering one's own advancement or best interests. Jonathan's own future role was at stake in Jonathan's case. David could have expanded his territory at Hanun's expense (as in the end he did). Barzillai might have played it safe by remaining neutral, or conceivably might even have approached Absalom. So too Hushai could have followed Ahithophel in genuine alliance with Absalom or at least could have avoided extraordinary risk by simply remaining with David.

These stories suggest also that loyalty in the biblical sense is not "company loyalty" in the sense of automatic loyalty to one's superior officer or employer. Rather, loyalty is invoked in terms of the serious need of the recipient, a need that places the recipient in a situation of weakness vis-à-vis the one acting loyally. The repercussions which we today often anticipate as consequences of failure to show company loyalty—the silent treatment, demotion, or even firing—are not much involved here, because without the called-for loyalty, the biblical recipient would probably be unable to retaliate.[11] Thus, as has already been emphasized, the preceding examples bring together a context of commitment and an occasion of free decision to carry forward that commitment.

## OTHER STORIES
## OF POLITICAL CONFLICT

### Spies at Jericho and Bethel

Other stories of political loyalty from the Deuteronomic history[12] present contexts and features somewhat divergent from the David stories. Particularly notable are the instances of Rahab and the spies (Joshua 2) and the parallel incident of the informer from the city of Bethel (Judg. 1:22–25). In each of these cases an inhabitant of a Canaanite city is said to show loyalty to an Israelite spying party by aiding in their takeover of the city. Rahab's "loyalty" (RSV "dealing kindly") is the hiding of the spies; they in turn offer her the loyalty of saving her family during the forthcoming attack on Jericho, providing she maintains their secret after they leave. The man from Bethel receives life for himself and his family in exchange for information about the town's fortification. But since the spies encounter the man outside the city, one has the impression that they may have held a considerable advantage which placed him under duress. These stories have been used to argue that the biblical concept of loyalty does not pertain to established relationships, but moves outside or beyond such relationships.[13] It is true that Nelson Glueck's effort[14] to focus on the host-guest relationship is weak in the case of Rahab and is surely forced in the Bethel case. I would suggest that in both incidents the relationship at stake is one of political identity, of siding with Israel over against the respective Canaanite compatriots.

Although Josh. 2:12–14 involves difficult textual problems,[15] the general picture of the conversation on Rahab's roof comes through. Here we have an "exchange" of acts of loyalty. In common parlance, Rahab proposes that "one good turn deserves another," although both acts involve life and death, not just some casual act of helpfulness. The proviso that Rahab must maintain the spies' secret (v. 14) is unique in the Old Testament as a condition placed upon a promise to do loyalty; usually a prior act or just the existence of a relationship seems to be the basis for loyalty, and no additional stipulations are set. There is some evidence that the conditional phrase "If you do not tell this business of ours" may be textually secondary; its omission would make this story more like other examples of loyalty. The insistence upon the condition, however, may reflect the unusual situation in which there is no history of relationship between the parties involved. The relationship comes into existence, in my view, through Rahab's recognition of Yahweh as God and her recognition that Yahweh has given Israel the land (vv. 8–11). Her action to save the spies, as well as Israel's subsequent saving of her and her family, is consequent upon this confession. It is the basis for her action in hiding the spies and in lying to the king's representatives.[16] The spies' condition of secrecy then simply requires that Rahab remain true to the relationship with Israel (not simply with the spies) which was implied by her words.

Insofar as Rahab believed her own statement about the God of Israel, she could be said to have acted out of enlightened self-interest. At the same time, the narrator surely intends us to sense the enormous risk she was taking in defying Jericho's king and his forces. Edgar Kellenberger is certainly correct that we do not have here a context of formal (covenant) relationship. Yet, to make a choice in a context of such great conflict implies a choice between relationships. Rahab chose for Israel. Much more than in the case of Jonathan, even more than in the case of Hanun, Rahab's choice marked a no-return decision. Here there could be no hope at all for any eventual reconciliation of the two sides.

In reflecting ethically upon such a story, we find that our first inclination is to discount Rahab's clarity about her options as editorial hindsight. In assessing our own loyalty, we tend to find that the right choice is rarely so easy to discern. We lack Rahab's certainty about what God has done and is doing. Certainly there is reality to be recognized both in our situational ambiguity and in the Bible's editorial hindsight. But we should take care not to let these realities blind us to the power of Rahab's decision. The narrator does not tell us anything of her struggle or lack thereof; but since Hebrew narrative so rarely mentions inner reflections, we may not automatically conclude that her decision was easily made. Even if she had theological clarity, the choice must have been difficult. Her life was at stake either way. Circumstances forced her hand, so that she had to decide quickly. By contrast, we are most often able to keep rearranging circumstances so that decisions can be postponed. But when the critical moment comes it still may not be easy to choose for faith. The testimony of Rahab's choice for Yahweh, even more than her assistance to Israel's cause, grants her a place of memory in the "roll call of the faithful" in Hebrews 11.

In the traditio-historically similar story of the man of Bethel in Judges 1, no relationship of any enduring kind is established between the parties. The man, once released by the Israelites, goes off to Hittite territory to establish his own town. It is in such a situation, however exceptional, that an inadequacy of our English word "loyalty" for conveying the Hebrew conception becomes apparent. The NAB's "spare you" simply supplies the content of the "loyal" action offered by the spies. The RSV's "deal kindly" seems too innocuous for sparing of life; Boling's "deal justly"[17] catches the flavor of the occasion so long as it is understood that it is a relational rather than a legal principle which is involved. "Uprightly" may convey the nuance here, but it should be noted that Hebrew has other vocabulary usually translated "just" or "upright" which is not being used here. What this incident shares with the Rahab story, and what the reference to loyalty probably intends to highlight, is the radical reversal of roles of freedom and dependence on the part of city dweller and spies. Without information from the Bethel resident the Israelite attack has little chance for success. They are dependent upon him. Once his information is given, he becomes, of course, theoretically expendable, hence dependent on the spies. Repeatedly we have seen that situations calling for loyalty involve full freedom of decision coupled with moral commitment to the person in need. The story of the man from Bethel meets this basic description even though our English word "loyalty" is not particularly apt for the specific context.

### Ahab and Ben-hadad

Similar in character is the incident recorded in 1 Kings 20:31–34. In the face of the Israelite rout of the Syrian forces, the advisers of the Syrian leader Ben-hadad suggest that he approach the king of Israel in humility and ask that his life be spared. The advice is given on the basis of the reputation of the kings of Israel as "merciful" (RSV). Ahab indeed accepts Ben-hadad's proposal of settlement terms favorable to Israel and lets his "brother" go free. In this case the RSV choice of "merciful" seems apt, although again Hebrew has a different word *(rḥm)* which more usually corresponds to this English word. English speakers simply are not accustomed to thinking of loyalty as a category relevant to relationships between military archenemies. Since the connection between the parties appears to be based only in hostility, mercy may seem the more appropriate rationale for explaining what happens in this story. But the narrative leaves much unsaid. Could Ahab have achieved the resulting economic and territorial hegemony for Israel if he had slain Ben-hadad?[18] Possibly not. Was the economic arrangement between their predecessors one made only under duress, or was it one involving mutual agreement and advantage? The text is not clear on this point. It does appear that despite the current warfare the narrator presupposes some prior history of relationship between heads of the two peoples. And even though the context is one of hostility, one characteristic feature of biblical loyalty is clearly present: appeal is made to one in power on behalf of one who is in desperate need. Only Ahab can deal with Ben-hadad's case. One may say at least that Ahab was loyal to his word. His reference to Ben-hadad as his "brother" could have been a ruse to flush out his enemy, but the reputation for loyalty of the kings of Israel was proved right as Ahab followed through by establishing a treaty.

Yet another point of tension must be noted in connection with this narrative. The release of Ben-hadad is followed by a strange incident in which a member of the prophetic guild condemns the king of Israel for freeing a man against God's will (1 Kings 20:35–43). Though none of the participants is named, the placement of this paragraph makes clear that it is intended as indictment of Ahab for what he has done. The important point is that the freeing of the Syrian king, which from an ordinary human view-point one would take to be an illustration of mercy/loyalty, is condemned as being against God's plan. At issue here is not an evaluation of Ahab's political decision by modern standards of politics and warfare or by modern views of the value of human life. On such grounds many readers might want to side with Ahab over against the prophet. The issue is, rather, the difficult and disturbing possibility that human and divine assessments of any given act of loyalty may not match. This story raises the possibility of misplaced or misdirected human loyalty.

In all of the examples considered thus far, the action of the loyal individual was viewed (at least implicitly) by the narrator as consonant with God's intention for the situation. The rightness of the loyalty shown usually seems self-evident to the Bible reader, given the benefit of the narrator's theological hindsight and knowledge of the final outcome of the story. But surely in the time of the event itself Hushai's loyalty seemed misplaced from Absalom's point of view; or Jonathan's from Saul's point of view; or Rahab's from the perspective of Jericho's ruler. Loyalty can regularly be viewed from a human perspective as misplaced. Since loyalty is so often tested out in situations of conflict, one cannot expect to find unanimous human approval for any action taken. But an act conceived of as loyal may also be misdirected from God's perspective. The incident of the anonymous prophet implies that Ahab should have known that his action was wrong. Yet the convicting parable with its picture of the captive slipping away through inattention leaves room for poor judgment rather than deliberate disobedience. Whether Ahab consciously and deliberately acted wrongly we are not told; his motives are simply not recorded. We know nothing of how he balanced out Israel's own welfare and its relationship with Syria in his decision. It is the possibility of error in judgment which is important to highlight here. Often enough Israel knew its duty and failed to do it (see chapter 5, "Loyalty: The Calling of the People of God"). But a story such as this one reminds us that life's choices are ambiguous, that our good intentions are not automatically in conformity with God's will. The reminder is not very comforting as we struggle with the choices that loyal living requires. Ahab was "resentful and sullen" after the prophet confronted him. We too often respond resentfully when challenged about our choices, especially when we need to admit we were wrong. Through this strange story we find that the choices were no easier for biblical folk than for ourselves, and that while good intentions are very important, they are not the ultimate standard for loyalty.

STORIES OF FAMILY RELATIONSHIPS

All of the stories considered to this point come from the world of politics and public affairs. Even the story of David and Jonathan was highly political, although it carried strong overtones of personal friendship as well. Loyalty is equally important, however, to the maintaining of relationships in the personal or private sphere of life. Three narratives will illustrate the many dimensions of continuity and some difference of nuance when loyalty is spoken of within the family setting. The most striking difference is that in the family the basis for loyalty is simply presumed. There is no appeal to the past history of the relationship or any previous acts of loyalty.

*Sarah and Abraham*

A prime example of a more personal act of loyalty involves Sarah and Abraham. The tradition of the "endangerment of the ancestress" appears three times in Genesis,[19] each with variations of emphasis and nuance. In each case the husband, fearful for his life, pretends his wife is his sister so that a foreign king will not kill him. The issue of loyalty comes up explicitly only in Gen. 20:13, where Abraham's request that Sarah present herself as his sister is portrayed as his request for loyal action on her part. In Genesis 20 this request is reported in the course of Abraham's explanation to Abimelech; in Genesis 12 the narrator recounts Abraham's actual address to Sarah (but without explicit reference to an act of loyalty). In the Genesis 20 tradition, Abraham presents a kinship picture which saves the sister-brother claim from complete falsehood, yet it is surely the fact of a conjugal bond which is being covered up in each instance.

In all three traditions it is the husband himself who actually says that the woman is his sister; in the ancient culture it would probably be usual for a man to be responsible for any woman in his household, regardless of the relationship. Thus the request to Sarah apparently involves her complicity in disguising the relationship, rather than any overt initiative on her part. In Genesis 20, Abimelech says that Sarah did confirm Abraham's statement, but otherwise Sarah has no role. The story is told from the male characters' point of view; except for the indirect quotation of 20:5, Sarah neither speaks nor takes any action in either of the accounts. Only at the conclusion of the second account does Abimelech address Sarah with concern for her honor in the entire affair.

From Abraham's point of view, Sarah's cooperation is an essential component of a plan to save his own life. She would be taken into the house of the foreign king in any event. At issue was only what would become of Abraham in the process—death or riches. Although from a sociocultural perspective Sarah was subordinate to her husband (brother), in this particular setting his life was in her hands. Because of their relationship she had a commitment to him, yet she was free to decide whether or not to perform the act of loyalty requested. So far as we can tell, her own fate would be the same in either case. Loyalty meant being less than completely truthful, for the sake of the other. Abraham asks this of her without any special pleading. It is as if the relationship itself provides whatever basis is necessary for his request.

It is often said that Abraham's action shows his lack of trust in God. Indeed, in Genesis 12 it is immediately following Yahweh's promise of many offspring that Abraham devises this plan to save himself. The man who set out from home not knowing where God would lead him seems suddenly to go into a panic. Does the story of Abraham's request and Sarah's compliance illustrate again human loyalty which is wrong or sinful in God's sight? Should Sarah have told the truth and trusted God? On careful examination, it seems that neither ancient narrator[20] had this question particularly in mind. The chief concern of each story is only to show that Sarah's purity was not compromised and that she was restored to Abraham—through divine intervention by plague or dream which reveals the true state of affairs to the foreign king. Neither Sarah nor Abraham is criticized by God; in fact, it is Abraham's prayer that restores fecundity to Abimelech's wife and female slaves. Disobedience is not explicitly at issue. But the elements of commitment, a critical need, freedom of decision, and moral choice are central to this event, just as in the political narratives considered earlier. Loyalty consists in doing what is right by the relationship, preserving alive that relationship even though circumstances present the opportunity to do otherwise with no human reprisal.

## Joseph and Jacob

These same characteristics may be seen in another incident in Genesis. The end of Genesis 47 records Israel's (Jacob's) deathbed request of his son Joseph that Jacob be buried with his ancestors, not in Egypt. Genesis 50 records Joseph's fulfilling of this request for loyalty. Although death at a ripe old age was viewed in most of Israel's history as a given, as natural, and although there was no cult of the dead in Israel,[21] the importance of a grave's location (in the homeland and with family) should not be underestimated. From Jacob's point of view the place of his burial was no casual matter; the amount of attention paid to burial location in various types of Old Testament literature underlines the depth of his concern.[22] Jacob's request fits with the characteristics of loyalty which have been observed in other passages. His need is important and he is unable to fulfill it himself (in this case by definition, since it will follow his death). Thus he is dependent upon someone else. Joseph as his son has a commitment to his father because of their relationship. Yet he also has freedom of decision; if he does not follow through, Jacob will have no recourse (being already dead) and there is no structure for community enforcement or reprisal. In this instance we find Jacob taking an additional measure to provide that Joseph will carry through. He asks Joseph to swear an oath (symbolized by placing his hand under his thigh) that he will take his father's body to Canaan. In taking the oath, Joseph makes himself specifically accountable before God. The oath heightens the general dimension of moral responsibility which is characteristic of biblical loyalty, for such swearing was done with radical seriousness; it was understood that God would bring judgment on anyone who failed to keep an oath.

This oath taking seems at first glance to short-circuit the freedom of decision which usually inheres in a situation in which loyalty is lived out. The one who is to show loyalty now will face drastic divine consequences rather than no social consequences if the relationship is not honored. But it has been the case regularly that a moral commitment (before God) is implied even when it is not made explicit. A divine response to faithful or unfaithful living may be presumed whether or not it is spelled out. From another perspective, the oath simply moves ahead the moment of decision to the immediate context of the request (so that agreeing to take the oath is tantamount to a "yes" decision about the request for loyalty).

From a comparison of other narratives where loyalty and oath taking come together, it appears that an oath may have been used when the act of loyalty would take place relatively further in the future, or in a situation of geographic separation, or otherwise beyond the possibility of renewed request. In the Rahab story discussed earlier, one might suppose that the connection between the parties was so fragile that the oath was used also to provide some assurance as to how matters would turn out. The language of the oath of loyalty sworn by Abraham to Abimelech in Gen. 21:23 is essentially the same as that found in the Rahab story, and the general conditions are similar. In each instance, parties formerly at enmity are in the process of entering into a positive relationship.[23] In the case of David and Jonathan (1 Samuel 20), however, David (or Jonathan) is pictured as reiterating a general oath of alliance which is understood to be the relational basis for loyalty. Here then the relationship itself is sworn to, rather than any particular action. A fifth instance of oath taking involves Abraham and his servant who journeys to seek a wife for Isaac (Genesis 24). The language for the oath taking there is like that of the Joseph case and presumably comes from the same narrator; however, the term "loyalty" is not explicitly incorporated into the oath; it is God's loyalty to Abraham which is the focus of the narrative.[24]

The variety of authors, periods, and narrative circumstances is wide enough that no narrow conclusion about the role of the oath should be drawn. Other examples of loyalty can be cited which involve geographic separation (Ben-hadad), enmity turned to friendship (the man from Bethel), or an extended time frame (David's deathbed request for Barzillai's sons) and yet lack an oath formula. The oath should therefore be viewed as an optional strengthening of the request or bond rather than a procedure mandated by certain circumstances. What is important is that the oath does not "cheapen" the loyalty shown by "forcing" the actor to live up to the relationship. Rather, it provides assurance which reinforces the underlying bond between those involved and serves to sustain the resolve of the oath taker in the face of various circumstances in which commitment might fade and loyalty be left undone.

As we will see in subsequent chapters, a chief difference between human and divine loyalty is that human loyalty tends characteristically to fade and waver even under the best of conditions, while divine loyalty grows ever stronger and surer even in the least favorable circumstances. The occasional use of the oath in these "secular" (i.e., not overtly religious) narratives about loyalty serves as reminder of the frailty of human will to do good and as pointer to the seriousness with which any promise of faithfulness should be undertaken.

In addition to the oath, Jacob's deathbed request includes one other feature which deserves special mention here. The RSV translation "loyally and truly" represents the Hebrew expression *ḥesed we'ĕmet*, a fixed expression used most often in connection with divine loyalty,[25] but occasionally concerning human loyalty also. Aside from a few passages in Proverbs (see esp. Prov. 3:3) where this double quality is described as much to be desired in human life style, the occurrences with human referent are only three in number: this Jacob-Joseph encounter; the words between Rahab and the spies; and the climactic conclusion of Abraham's servant's speech to Laban concerning the betrothal of Rebekah ("Now then, if you will deal loyally and truly with my master, tell me; and if not, tell me," Gen. 24:49).[26]

It will be seen immediately that the oath taking overlaps this narrative usage, with an oath being in the foreground in the Jacob and Rahab examples, and in the background for this third story. Although Genesis 24 involves loyalty to be shown by Laban to his kinsman Abraham, the servant is under an oath to Abraham, to be freed from it only if the woman (v. 8) or her kindred (v. 41) refuse to cooperate in his mission. The characteristics of the oath situation—need for clear decision (for the servant's sake), inability of the party in need (Abraham) through time or geography to pursue the request—are operative here as well.

In this idiomatic expression *ḥesed we'ĕmet*, "loyalty" and "truth" are not to be regarded as two separate qualities to be shown. Rather, as has often been suggested, the noun "truth" (better, "faithfulness" or "trustworthiness") here functions by hendiadys to qualify the basic notion of loyalty. That qualifying is clearly a strengthening of some sort,[27] just as the oath strengthens the likelihood of living faithfully in the situations where it is invoked. In circumstances that pertain to behavior over an extended period of time, the nuancing of "faithful loyalty" may emphasize constancy. In cases such as these three narratives where a specific decision or action is in view, the focus is more (as with the oath) on being sure to carry through on the particular matter. This kind of qualification might be expressed in English by a verbal or an adverbial construction such as, "If you are definitely going to deal loyally," or "Be sure to show loyalty."

Again, as with the oath, a request that uses the longer expression should not be construed to cast aspersion on the good intention of the person asked to live faithfully. (Note that the spies *offer* Rahab their "sure loyalty.") The expression functions positively, lifting up the importance of the need being filled, the value of the relationship, and the entrusting of the need to the care of the one who is to act loyally. These themes taken together serve to underline strongly the basic conception of loyalty itself, the free taking up of one's relational obligation in a situation of special need.

### Ruth and Naomi

Near the climax of the Book of Ruth, Boaz invokes God's blessing upon Ruth, saying:

> You have made your latter loyalty better than the former in not going after [the] young men, whether poor or rich. (Ruth 3:10, au. trans.)

The scene is the threshing floor; Ruth has just pointed out Boaz's legal position as "redeemer" and has by her actions invited him to marry her in fulfillment of that responsibility. The fine commentary of E. F. Campbell on this chapter highlights the craft of the narrator in this passage replete with suspense and double-entendre.[28] The surface question of whether sexual intercourse will ensue points to the larger and more serious question of whether the whole matter of widowhood and kinship will be resolved uprightly, as it ought to be in Israel. Ruth the Moabite woman is portrayed as the example of what loyal Israelite living ought to be like. Hers is the initiative; she not only sets the stage but also tells Boaz what his role should be. Her loyalty then is not just to Naomi (though that is primary) but also to her dead husband, dead brother-in-law, dead father-in-law—indeed, to the whole family of which she became a part through her marriage. Her "former" loyalty consisted in standing by her mother-in-law, Naomi, in coming to the strange land of her dead husband. Her "latter" loyalty follows through on the former in her initiative to provide an heir for Naomi (see 4:14, 17) and economic security for both of them within the structure of the system of levirate marriage.[29]

As in so many previous examples, the decision about the future of the relationship lay entirely in the hands of one of the persons involved. Ruth might have followed Naomi's original advice and her sister-in-law Orpah's example and returned to her own (Moabite) family; and Boaz implies that once in Israel, Ruth might have sought out a more convenient or promising alliance. The choices which affected the other persons, living and dead, belonged to Ruth; no coercion or social pressure was part of the picture.

While giving due attention to the narrator's presentation of Ruth as a paragon of faithful living, it is appropriate that we pause to consider the situation of Orpah. Often Orpah is looked down upon for deserting Naomi in contrast to the faithful Ruth, even though Naomi herself suggested the leave-taking (albeit in words reflecting the bitterness, anguish, and futility of her situation, not in any constructive attitude). But it is important to note that the narrator has no word of judgment against Orpah. It was not necessarily a failure of loyalty to close out a relationship under certain circumstances. Rather, Orpah's decision highlights the extraordinary loyalty of Ruth. The narrative suggests that biblical faithful living involves matters of degree, not simply the presence or absence of loyalty. This perspective reinforces the observation made earlier that loyalty is a quality that may wax or wane. Recognizing degrees of loyalty also helps to account for the wide range of actions that can be described under the rubric of loyalty—acts easy to do and acts involving very great risk; acts in accord with one's self-interest and acts that seem contrary to the best interest of the actor.

The Ruth narrative itself signals to us that Orpah's decision should not be regarded as disloyal. The clue lies in the way in which Naomi puts the suggestion of leave-taking to her daughters-in-law:

> May Yahweh show you the same loyalty which you have shown to the
> dead and to me. (Ruth 1:8, au. trans.)

From Naomi's point of view, indeed from the common-sense point of view of the ancient reader (and perhaps the modern one as well), a parting of ways is sensible and practical, given the deaths of all three men of the family. Naomi can do no more for her daughters-in-law, since there are no more sons for them to marry.[30] So she urges that they return to their Moabite families and eventually remarry. Since Naomi is no longer in a position to do anything on behalf of the relationship, she commits the two women to God's keeping. The words that she uses sound like a general wish, but it is quite possible that they give us a glimpse of a formula by which to bring a good relationship to an end with no recrimination or disloyalty on either side. In asking God to do what she cannot do, Naomi signals Ruth and Orpah that they stand free of any further commitment. Orpah's decision is thus appropriate, not disloyal. Loyalty does not require continuation of every relationship at any cost. Orpah's proper decision helps the narrator to show the reader how extraordinary Ruth's loyalty really is.

Another instance of this "benedictory" invocation of divine loyalty appears in the David narrative of 2 Sam. 15:20. A large entourage of supporters seeks to accompany David in his flight from Absalom's insurgency; among these is the man Ittai. Ittai, from the Philistine city of Gath, is a foreigner who has been only briefly in David's service. David urges Ittai and his six hundred men to take their leave, since he knows nothing of what the future holds; he concludes his exhortation with the words, "May Yahweh be sure to show loyalty to you." Again a person in dire straits uses the phrase as a way of releasing the other from responsibility and thus bringing the relationship to an honorable conclusion. As in the case of Naomi and Orpah, here too the person in need does not commit *himself* to God's care as a way to excuse the other; rather, it is the *other* for whom God's loyalty is prayed. The assumption is that roles cannot again be reversed, so that loyalty received can never again be reciprocated. Yahweh is asked to do that which David and Naomi cannot see any way to do themselves. Ittai and Ruth show the depth of their faithfulness in their refusal to accept this opportunity to lay down the commitments they have undertaken.

These references to divine loyalty in the stories of Naomi and David provide a fitting transition to a broader discussion of the loyalty of God. Each comes in a context that highlights a remark-

able degree of human loyalty, yet each points to the critical importance of sure divine loyalty in the midst of the ebb and flow of
human power and human relationships. Moreover, each suggests
the extension of Yahweh's loyalty beyond the formal bounds of
Israel. The next two chapters will consider Yahweh's loyalty to the
Israelite community and to its individual members within the
larger framework of divine loyalty to all the world.

## NOTES

1. P. Kyle McCarter, Jr., *I Samuel*, AB 8 (Garden City, N.Y.: Doubleday & Co., 1980), 18–30.
2. Possibly the Deuteronomic historian. Cf., e.g., McCarter, *I Samuel*, 16, 342, 344. These verses anticipate the Mephibosheth incident of
2 Samuel 9, in which the theme of loyalty is recapitulated (see pp. 13–15).
3. Nearly every story to be discussed in this chapter will relate loyalty
to a very dramatic situation of need. This reflects a natural tendency of
narrative to concentrate on dramatic events. Fulfilling of "small" needs is
equally a part of living loyally; the point is that the need is serious,
whatever it is, and that its fulfillment strengthens the relationship. See
chap. 5, "Loyalty: The Calling of the People of God," and chap. 6,
"Review and Reflection."
4. Michael Fishbane, "The Treaty Background of Amos 1:11 and
Related Matters," *JBL* 89 (1970):314. This vocabulary of love has sometimes been taken to allude to a homosexual relationship between the two
men; see, for example, Tom Horner, *Jonathan Loved David* (Philadelphia:
Westminster Press, 1978). The reference to kissing in 1 Sam. 20:41 and
David's comparison of Jonathan's love to the love of women (2 Sam. 1:26)
are usually cited. Yet the kiss is certainly open to a more general meaning,
and the comparison to love of women appears to be a poetic device
analogous to Naomi's friends' assessment of Ruth who "loved" her, as
"more to you than seven sons." See my treatment of these texts in "Loyalty
and Love: The Language of Human Interconnections in the Hebrew
Bible," *Michigan Quarterly Review* 27 (1983): 190–204.
5. Since the English word "loyalty" seems so automatically to imply
some existing relationship, the point may seem labored. But there are a
few biblical texts where it is not so clear (notably the spies and the man of
Bethel [Judg. 1:22–26] and the story of Rahab [Joshua 2]). The significance of an existing relationship and the question of whether loyalty
merely conforms to or instead presses beyond the bounds of any such

relationship have been classic issues in the technical debate over the meaning of Hebrew *ḥesed*.

6. For a hint of the problems involved, compare the RSV and NAB translations. For more detailed analysis, see McCarter, *I Samuel*, 336–37, and my own *The Meaning of Ḥesed in the Hebrew Bible*, HSM 17 (Missoula, Mont.: Scholars Press, 1978), 85–87. If we follow McCarter's view that the paragraph of 1 Sam. 20:12–17 is an interpolation, then Jonathan's consideration of his possible death anticipates not only the risk of Saul's wrath against him for helping David (cf. 1 Sam. 20:33) but also Jonathan's actual death at Mt. Gilboa.

7. Whether Jonathan went so far as to make David swear (1 Sam. 20:17) is doubtful, as a comparison of translations will show. It is equally likely that Jonathan reiterated his own oath rather than exacting one from David.

8. The sequence of David's takeovers is not certain. Second Samuel 8 seems to be a summary review which covers the defeat of Syria (attributed here in 2 Samuel 10 to Syria's support of Ammon) but makes no mention of a Syrian-Ammonite alliance. David's military potential would be known from his internal exploits, in any case.

9. Absalom had fled to an Aramean territory under David's control after killing his brother Amnon in retaliation for Amnon's violating their sister Tamar (2 Samuel 13). The story of David's family is filled with tragedy as well as glory.

10. The term "friend" may allude to the title "king's friend," which apparently referred to a special royal adviser in the court of the United Monarchy. See 1 Kings 4:5; 1 Chron. 27:33. Possibly the narrator here intends both the technical term and an emphasis on Hushai's true friendship to David seen in his risky act of loyalty.

11. Hanun, of course, got into trouble with David. But Hanun's downfall stemmed from his unwillingness to accept the loyalty which was offered to him. He initiated a military solution to his situation, and David responded in kind.

12. Whether from a first or second historian or from their sources does not affect the discussion here.

13. So Edgar Kellenberger, *ḥäsäd wä'ᵃmät als Ausdruck einer Glaubenserfahrung*, ATANT 69 (Zurich: Theologischer Verlag, 1982), 118–20.

14. Nelson Glueck, *Ḥesed in the Bible* (Cincinnati: Hebrew Union College Press, 1967; German original, Giessen: Töpelmann, 1927), 44.

15. Contrast the RSV translation with that of R. G. Boling, *Joshua*, AB 6 (Garden City, N.Y.: Doubleday & Co., 1982), 140, and see Boling's textual notes. See also the textual notes in my *Meaning of Ḥesed*, 64–68.

16. In the narrative sequence, Rahab declares her view of Yahweh and

Israel only after she has acted; but her statement is explained to have been chronologically prior: "Before they lay down, she came up to them on the roof, and said . . ." (Josh. 2:8).

17. R. G. Boling, *Judges*, AB 6A (Garden City, N.Y.: Doubleday & Co., 1975), 52.

18. The historical details of this entire incident are much discussed in the literature. See, e.g., J. Maxwell Miller, *The Old Testament and the Historian* (Philadelphia: Fortress Press, 1976), 20–39. The exact dating and the precise identity of the antagonists are not essential to our consideration of loyalty in the historian's summary of the event.

19. Abraham, Sarah, and the Pharaoh of Egypt, Genesis 12; Abraham, Sarah, and Abimelech of Gerar, Genesis 20; Rebecca, Isaac, and Abimelech, Genesis 26.

20. J in Genesis 12, E in Genesis 20, according to traditional source-critical analysis. The whole matter of sources in Genesis is now being reassessed by some scholars. See, e.g., Rolf Rendtorff, *Das über-lieferungsgeschichtliche Problem des Pentateuch*, BZAW 147 (New York: Walter de Gruyter, 1976). But the matter of sources is not critical to the discussion here, as the concept of loyalty has never been suggested to shift in its usage between J and E. One does need to be cautious methodologically about importing any material from a parallel text that would by conflation substantively change the narrative which speaks of loyalty.

21. See Lloyd R. Bailey, Sr., *Biblical Perspectives on Death* (Philadelphia: Fortress Press, 1979).

22. The attention to locations of the graves of Sarah (Genesis 23), Rachel (Genesis 35), Joshua, Joseph, and Eleazar (Joshua 24), the recovery and burial of the corpses of Saul and Jonathan (1 Sam. 31:11–13, cf. 2 Sam. 2:4b–6, where Saul's burial is treated as an act of loyalty, and 2 Sam. 21:11–14), and prophetic material such as Jer. 22:18–19 or Isa. 14:18–20 are but some of the indicators of this concern for place of burial.

23. This text has not been discussed in detail. The aim of the chapter is to present representative samples rather than exhaustive coverage.

24. See chap. 4, "Help in Need," 91.

25. See the discussion in chap. 3, "Freedom and Commitment," 57–60.

26. No clear pattern of usage of this idiom by author or tradition can be discerned; see my *Meaning of Ḥesed*, 32–33.

27. It is quite possible that since the longer phrase became a fixed expression, it was used simply as a variant for the single word, perhaps for emphasis, but without a clear purpose to say something different.

28. E. F. Campbell, *Ruth*, AB 7 (Garden City, N.Y.: Doubleday & Co., 1975), 130–38. See also the sensitive treatment of Ruth by Phyllis Trible, *God and the Rhetoric of Sexuality* (Philadelphia: Fortress Press, 1978), 166–99.

29. See Thomas and Dorothy Thompson, "Some Legal Problems in the Book of Ruth," *VT* 18 (1968): 79–99.

30. Naomi apparently has no home kinfolk in mind at this point. The narrator does not explain why she remembers Boaz's relationship only after Ruth gleans in his fields. The plot form allows the mysterious ways of God's providing through faithful people to be highlighted.

CHAPTER 3

# Freedom and Commitment: God's Covenant Loyalty

O give thanks to the Lord, for he is good,
for his loyalty endures for ever.
                                                            (Ps. 136:1)

This chapter and the next explore the character of divine loyalty, traditionally translated "mercy" in this familiar hymnic refrain of the psalms. The refrain indicates one characteristic of divine loyalty which sets it apart from the human loyalty which has been described in chapter 2, "Stories of Human Loyalty": God's loyalty is permanent, it "endures for ever." Although divine loyalty may be prayed for urgently, there is the sense in Israel that it can be counted upon. There is not the fear or risk, attendant upon human relationships, that loyalty will prove too difficult, costly, or unattractive to Yahweh. The pressing question is whether loyalty might be withdrawn because of sin.

God's loyalty to the people of Israel as the sacred community, the elect people of God, will be the focus of this chapter, which centers upon the place of loyalty in Israel's covenantal conceptions of its relationship to Yahweh. Chapter 4, "Help in Need," will then describe ways in which this divine loyalty to the community takes shape in relation to specific needs of the community and of its individual members.

In reflecting upon the various aspects of human loyalty which emerged from the study of narratives in the preceding chapter, we see clearly that this concept of loyalty is full of power to express the nature of Israel's God in relationship to the people. Divine loyalty, to be sure, is not simply human loyalty writ large. God shows loyalty in ways that challenge and correct the inadequacies of human expressions of commitment. Yet God language is anthropomorphic, as has been emphasized in chapter 1, "Introduction: Contemporary Experience and Ancient Witness." It is through this continuity of conceptual language that we may grasp much of what Israel had in mind in speaking of Yahweh's loyalty.

In chapter 2, "Stories of Human Loyalty," we have seen that the association of personal obligation with the practical or situational freedom to ignore that obligation lies at the foundation of Israel's understanding of occasions for human loyalty. Theologically speaking, this word loyalty can then evoke in a single breath both the commitment of God to the community of faith and the radical freedom of the One who can in no way be coerced by the people with whom relationship has been established. So the people pray and God responds, but the response is based in divine commitment, not in necessity. To speak of God as free yet bound, and to insist that God's action toward the people stems as much from the freedom as from the boundness, is a paradox that is basic to biblical faith. For Israel, "loyalty" was the word that expressed this paradox.

Beyond this holding together of free decision and obligation, the Israelite concept of loyalty also incorporated the idea of aid provided for another who was in extreme need. Theologically, Israel is always pictured as dependent upon Yahweh for its very existence as a community. It is in Yahweh's being with them that they have identity (Exod. 33:12–17), in Yahweh's strength they survive all the vicissitudes of their life as a political entity. Thus divine loyalty may be viewed generally as the very basis for Israel's life. There is also special appeal to God in times of community distress. Appeal to God implies in and of itself that human aid may fall short, that the situation lies in Yahweh's hands. So loyalty is the basis for specially recognized succor as well as for general sustenance. Freedom, commitment, and help in need are the parameters of Israel's view of Yahweh's loyalty to the community, loyalty which is made manifest in the context of covenant.

In chapter 2, "Stories of Human Loyalty," we have seen that the term "covenant" (Hebrew *bĕrît*) is sometimes used in connection with the exercise of loyalty to another person. Examples included David and Jonathan and Ben-hadad and Ahab.[1] A central problem in these cases and also in the following theological discussion is the relationship between loyalty and covenant. Which is the over-arching category? The debate is an old one, complicated as much by differing perspectives on covenant as by differing interpretations of loyalty. Most recently, Edgar Kellenberger has suggested that covenant is focused on legal duty; the existence of the weaker party is at stake in any breach of covenant (duty). Loyalty, he argues, is by contrast a more general notion, something that can be present in differing degrees. If it is strong, loyalty can outlast disobedience; if it is weak, it can fade away despite any formal contract or covenant. Since loyalty is the broader category, according to Kellenberger, loyalty was not confined to formal (covenant) relationships but could provide a basis for moving into such relationships. Genesis 21 and 1 Kings 20 are viewed as key examples.[2]

The issue can be sharpened by separating two component questions: First, is loyalty done apart from formal relationships (as well as within them)? And second, when loyalty is shown within relationships, does it encompass the expected, or the extraordinary, or both?

With regard to the first questions, I have tried to show that in the biblical perspective loyalty is a quality that is demonstrated within a relationship, not an action that brings a relationship into existence.[3] Thus, when Kellenberger speaks of loyalty as "presupposition" *(Voraussetzung)* of a covenant, I would concur insofar as he means that loyalty may have been shown before the pact was sworn to. But I would be very cautious about associating the swearing of the covenant with the beginning of the relationship itself, even in the Abraham and Abimelech narrative.[4] Loyalty is not restricted to any *one* kind of relationship, such as covenant, but conceptually it cannot be taken out of *some* context of relationship; it is shown within relationship.

The second question concerns the nature of what counts as loyalty in the biblical perspective. Nelson Glueck in his classic work emphasized the mutual exercise of rights and duties within a relationship, thus highlighting the relational aspect but seeking to focus on the expectedness or nonextraordinary quality of loyal living.[5] Other scholars have tried from various perspectives to question the "obligation" focus of Glueck's work, thus moving toward loyalty as something extraordinary within the relational context. The "extraordinary" character of loyalty has been seen in its tendency toward mercy or generosity[6] and also in the suggestion that many of the actions which we know in narrative as loyalty seem to go "beyond the call of duty" (at least as we modern folk see the matter).[7]

The discussion of examples of human loyalty in chapter 2, "Stories of Human Loyalty," has suggested that it is the combination of commitment in relationship, critical need of the recipient, and circumstantial freedom of the actor which characterize occasions for the exercise of loyalty. Recognition of this *combination* of elements shows that both Glueck and his critics grasped part of what was important but tended to use the part to override other important dimensions. Kellenberger is on the right track in de-emphasizing the legal aspects of rights and duties in order to emphasize hope for ongoing loyalty as foundational;[8] but he still, in my view, underestimates the force of commitment to the relationship as a source rather than only a consequence of loyalty.

It has been important to make this last point about loyalty as both ordinary (expected because of obligation or commitment) and extraordinary (sometimes going beyond what seems reasonable to ask of a commitment) in order to assess its place in Israel's covenant theology. For it is widely agreed that in Israel's own reflection there were two general models of covenant thinking, usually referred to as the Sinaitic (or Mosaic) and the Davidic. Within these two patterns, the Sinaitic tends to focus more on the extraordinary character of Yahweh's loyalty to Israel, while the Davidic turns more on the expected character of that loyalty.[9]

THE MOSAIC COVENANT TRADITION:
FREEDOM

The principal formulation of the Mosaic covenant tradition occurs in Exodus 19—24, the Old Epic (JE) account of the making of the covenant at Mt. Sinai. Efforts to show a neat correspondence between parts of this narrative and the structure of Hittite suzerainty treaties of the second millennium B.C. have not met with success.[10] Nonetheless, the case for the suzerainty treaty as the basic metaphor underlying the covenant related in this narrative is widely accepted. In such a treaty a suzerain or overlord binds a vassal to himself on the basis of previous acts of good will, generosity, or protection which that suzerain has done on behalf of the vassal or the vassal's forebears. The vassal is to agree to keep certain treaty stipulations (sole loyalty, military aid, and the like) and will receive blessing for obedience but cursing for disobedience. Deities are named as witnesses, presumably with the task of enforcing the blessings and the curses.[11] Many other passages—such as Joshua 24, much of Deuteronomy, and various psalms and prophetic passages—reflect this Mosaic covenant tradition as well.

### Conditional Loyalty

The Exodus 19—24 narrative incorporates other important material, most notably the theophany to all Israel. But for our purposes what is important is to see the legal material of this section (the Decalogue in Exodus 20 and the so-called covenant code which follows in 20:22—23:33) in relation to the stipulations of the treaty tradition. In the midst of the Decalogue, almost as if in passing, comes Yahweh's own assertion of the theme of blessing and curse,[12] protection and judgment, as it is understood in the core Mosaic tradition:

> For I the Lord your God am a jealous God, visiting the iniquity of the fathers upon the children to the third and the fourth generation of those who hate me, but showing loyalty to thousands of those who love me and keep my commandments. (Exod. 20:5b–6 = Deut. 5: 9b–10)

An examination of the immediate context and other related passages, however, will make clear that these potent words are anything but "in passing" in this setting. Their incorporation within the context of the Decalogue (both the Exodus 20 and Deuteronomy versions) meant that over the centuries they had extensive liturgical use; this recitation extended their community shaping power far beyond that of other parts of the narrative.

The words as we receive the Decalogue are attached to the prohibition of "bowing down and serving," which was originally connected with the "other gods" of Exod. 20:3 (rather than with graven images). The title of Yahweh as "jealous" is therefore specifically associated with the divine suzerain's right to exclusive obedience and worship from vassal Israel. The introduction to the Decalogue (viewed in Judaism as the First Commandment) prepares us for this demand for exclusive allegiance: "I am Yahweh your God, who brought you out of the land of Egypt." Although Dennis McCarthy rightly suggests that one should not try to read the Decalogue as a document modeled literarily on a Hittite treaty form,[13] it is still appropriate to see the political world view of such treaties as an analogy by which the theological significance of the Decalogue would be interpreted in Israel. The gracious deliverance given the community by its suzerain is the basis for the divine demand for obedience to the stipulations. Future relationships between Yahweh and Israel are dependent upon how Israel responds to the commands. And the setting of the options ("visiting the iniquity" versus "showing loyalty") is appropriately tied to the commandment of "no other gods," for only as Israel cleaves to Yahweh will it have any possibility of fulfilling the rest of the law.[14]

What this Mosaic covenant requires of Israel is often referred to as "exclusive loyalty" to the divine suzerain. But it is best to avoid for the moment the use of the word "loyalty" for Israel's obligation to God, since it may carry connotations inappropriate to the biblical perspective. (The nature of Israel's loyalty will be discussed in chapter 5, "Loyalty: The Calling of the People of God.") It is important to see that here in the Decalogue the text speaks of God's loyalty to Israel, not vice versa. And here loyalty is promised only for the obedient. The vocabulary of loving and hating is conspicuously political terminology in the context of ancient Near Eastern diplomacy.[15] To love is not merely to have a certain emotional attitude; rather, it is to live in such a way as to keep the terms of the covenant. For such a people Yahweh will show loyalty.

Loyalty will take shape in the protection of the faithful community from disaster.

Deuteronomy, a book whose structure corresponds in many respects to the suzerainty treaty form, gives some concreteness to our picture of the Israelite community as beneficiary of divine loyalty. Obedient Israel will become a great people who dwell secure in the land of promise. Moses exhorts Israel to be careful to do the command, so that "you may live and multiply, and go in and possess the land which the Lord swore to give to your fathers" (Deut. 8:1), "a land in which you will eat bread without scarcity" (v. 9). A community life of *shalom* (wholeness) springs forth as the manifestation of God's loyalty to Israel. The ancestral promises of increased numbers and settled territory symbolize Israel's basic conception of God's loyalty to the community within this Sinai covenant tradition. For a community whose self-identity was shaped by a memory of slavery, the freedom implied in independent and expanding family life and a place of bondage to no one would form the heart of a vision of *shalom*.[16]

In a setting of strong emphasis on obedience, the Decalogue says nothing of forgiveness; it speaks only of loyalty for the obedient, disaster for those who are disobedient. This emphasis is consistent with the import of blessings and curses in treaty tradition generally, and it is also appropriate to a liturgical context in which the community is being faced with the basic expectations laid before it by the deity. In the narrative of Exodus the people promise at the outset to be obedient (Exod. 19:8) even before they have heard the commandments of God given in Exodus 20—23. While there are surely redactional issues to be considered here,[17] the people's precipitate words still symbolize the difficulty of taking the will of God with radical seriousness. We, like ancient Israel, are often eager to be on board, ready to pledge ourselves to God even before we realize fully what is required. And such enthusiasm, such readiness to be beneficiaries of divine loyalty, is not ill founded. When the Israelites finally hear all the stipulations from Moses they repeat their initial promise, "All the words which the Lord has spoken we will do" (Exod. 24:3). The uncompromising threat and promise of the Decalogue stand as reminders to all that such commitments are not to be undertaken lightly.

Jeremiah 16:1–13 portrays in devastating terms the consequences of Israel's disobedience. Here Jeremiah is commanded by God to live a life of celibacy and even to avoid participating in funeral lamentations, as signs of the impending judgment of God. Then come the awful (awe-ful) words:

> For I have taken away my peace from this people, says the Lord, my loyalty and my mercy. (Jer. 16:5b)

The absence of loyalty is pictured here as life without gladness, death without mourning, and exile to an unknown land. Loyalty will be taken away, so that this fate befalls the people, because they "have gone after other gods and have served and worshiped them, and have forsaken me and have not kept my law" (v. 11). The allusion to the opening commandments of the Decalogue is conspicuous here. The threatened word of judgment of the Decalogue will come to pass. Jeremiah 16 stands alone in all of the Old Testament in its direct pronouncement of the end of divine loyalty to Israel. Although the passage is brief and in prose, the power of this section is comparable to that of Jer. 4:23–28, where God's judgment is seen in a vision of return to the "waste and void" of primeval chaos. For God's people, life without loyalty would surely be waste and void.

The picture in Jer. 16:5–13 is so stark as to be almost unbearable; vv. 14–15 suddenly introduce a promise of eventual restoration, apparently borrowed editorially from 23:7–8. This juxtaposition of restoration with judgment raises the question of how the Sinai covenant tradition actually functioned theologically. If the stark Decalogue restriction of loyalty to the obedient community had been the only word, then Jeremiah's pronouncement came centuries late. The covenant tradition announces curses for disobedience; in principle, any disobedience abrogates the covenant. Yet there must have been some provision for coping with the reality of disobedience, else the Sinai theology would not have survived. After all, the tradition reports that the people fell into sin even before they left the base of Mt. Sinai, in the matter of the golden calf. How is it that God did not bring final judgment and end the covenant relationship long before Jeremiah's time?

*Forgiving Loyalty*

A key to this question lies precisely within the framework of that golden calf narrative of the first disobedience. Despite many points of literary and traditio-historical unevenness,[18] the Old Epic tradition of Exodus 32—34 presents a coherent story line: During Moses' absence at the top of the mountain the people grow anxious and prevail upon Aaron to take their gold and make an image which is referred to as "your gods [sic] who brought you up out of the land of Egypt" and before which an altar is built. The language used for the ceremonial event at the altar plays upon the language of the covenant-sealing ritual of Exodus 24. Yahweh sees the people's action and becomes enraged and seeks to destroy the people entirely. But there follows a series of intercessions by Moses, with the general result that there is limited punishment, but total annihilation is averted. Yet God refuses to accompany the people in their departure from Sinai toward the promised land. Moses makes his last and most critical plea to God, and in response he is given a new copy of the commandments and a personal theophany. It is in this theophany that we find the classic Old Testament liturgical exposition of the name of God; and it is on the basis of that name that a renewed covenant is granted in response to Moses' final plea for the people's pardon.

As Moses stands in the cleft of the rock and God's glory passes by, he hears God's voice proclaiming:

> a God merciful and gracious,
> slow to anger, and abounding in loyalty and faithfulness,
> keeping loyalty for thousands,
> forgiving iniquity and transgression and sin,
> but who will by no means clear the guilty,
> visiting the iniquity of the fathers upon the children
>     and the children's children,
> to the third and the fourth generation.
>             (Exod. 34:6b–7, versification mine)

The printed arrangement of the text above is intended to emphasize the poetic character of this proclamation. Although such a full text appears only here, the repeated incorporation of its opening lines in the psalms and elsewhere suggests its extended liturgical use in Israel's worship.

In this proclamation of God's manner of relating to Israel the elements of loyalty and judgment which appear in the Decalogue are given a larger setting. The "jealous God" is also "God merciful and gracious."[19] Yahweh still appears as the One who "shows [here "keeps"] loyalty" and "visits iniquity." But the concept of loyalty is expanded by the addition of the phrase "forgiving iniquity and transgression and sin." The occasion of the golden calf is one of deepest affront to the deity—a turning to other gods; but this theophanic response opens the door to the possibility that the relationship between Yahweh and Israel can continue. In this setting one can begin to grasp the overwhelming importance of divine loyalty for Israel's faith. Here in the golden calf context forgiveness is included as a dimension of divine loyalty; because such forgiveness implies restoration of wholeness to the relationship, it can even be viewed as the basis for all the other manifestations of God's loyalty.

The basic options within the Mosaic covenant theology were simply existence or nonexistence of the people. After seeing the calf, God proposed to wipe the people out and start over with Moses (Exod. 32:10). Moses' intercession was followed by the death of some of the community by sword and by plague, yet Yahweh's refusal to accompany the people amounted to nonexistence for the entire people. As Moses put it, God's presence was that which made this people a people distinct from all others (33:16). The stamp of relationship to the suzerain was the cornerstone of Israel's identity. There was no possibility of changing allegiance to some other deity and still being Israel. And an angel intermediary, offered to make up for the withdrawing of divine presence, was no satisfactory substitute. Better to forget the promised land, to end the relationship completely. The sin of the vassal brings the relationship to the point of abrogation. But in the theophany the way back from the brink is given. Sin is not taken lightly, the guilty are not cleared (declared to be innocent when they are not), and judgment comes. But judgment is not the last word. Because of Yahweh's *abounding* loyalty, Israel continues as vassal before the suzerain.

The expression "abounding in loyalty" is used in the Old Testament only of God, never of human beings. It is especially this greatness of God's loyalty that distinguishes it from human loyalty, which is often by contrast characterized as frail or fickle.[20]. This distinction corresponds to the observation that in the Old Testament, human loyalty is never associated with forgiveness; only divine loyalty extends that far in its will to maintain relationship. The opening two lines of the Exodus 34 liturgical formula appear in a series of contexts which repeatedly connect the expression "abounding in loyalty" with divine forgiveness. In its liturgical association with "slow to anger," this nuance is reinforced.

Ezra's prayer,[21] for instance, links loyalty and forgiveness even more explicitly than the set formula of Exodus:

> But thou art a God ready to forgive, gracious and merciful, slow to anger and abounding in loyalty, and didst not forsake them. (Neh. 9:17b)

This prayer, like some of the psalms, incorporates a lengthy recitation of Israel's history as the people of God. Like Psalm 106 or Psalm 78 (but here in Nehemiah in prose form), the prayer focuses upon the interplay between Israel's disobedience and Yahweh's repeated unwillingness finally to forsake the people. The reference to abounding or abundant loyalty comes precisely in the context of recalling the desire to return to Egypt and the making of the golden calf. Composed centuries after Exodus 32—34, Ezra's prayer indicates the symbolic power of the old tradition of the calf as the basis of hope for God's forgiveness. Here that hope stretches even beyond the exile to a people who, though restored to the land itself, view themselves as slaves within that land (Neh. 9:36). And so in repentance they covenant (v. 38) to keep Moses' commands, in confident trust that the abundantly loyal God will improve their lot.

The same theme appears in Joel 2:13. Here the liturgical lines are used as the basis for a call to "return to the Lord, your God," to "rend your hearts and not your garments." The abounding loyalty of God offers confidence that a prayer for deliverance from approaching disaster will be heard when it comes from a penitent community. The dramatic picture of the locust plague and of the devastating "day of the Lord" which precedes the call to repentance suggests once again the concreteness of Israel's understanding of judgment and forgiveness. As in the Ezra story, but even more dramatically in Joel, forgiveness would be embodied in divine rescue of a helpless folk from overpowering trouble.

Finally, we find these poetic lines quoted in the Book of Jonah. Here the words may function more powerfully than anywhere else, for here Jonah spits them out against God in great anger. Because he *knew* that God was so gracious, merciful, patient, and loyal, says Jonah, *therefore* he fled from God's command to preach to Nineveh. Because God has turned out to be (as Jonah feared) so gracious, merciful, patient, and loyal, Jonah wants to die. For because God was so loyal, the Ninevites' repentance has been heard, and the city has not been destroyed. So poor Jonah is furious, because he is discredited (in his own eyes) as a prophet of God and because he cannot find it in himself to share God's pity for an enemy people.

This Jonah passage is important in several respects. First, it points beyond the confines of the Mosaic (or Davidic) covenant; here is one of the important Old Testament suggestions that God's loyalty is for all people, not only for Israel. It is possible that the writer has simply quoted from the liturgical tradition without much thought. But I find it more likely that the quotation is deliberately chosen to highlight the point of the story: God is not only judge of all nations but also One who cares for all nations, not just for Israel. The theme of forgiveness of all serves as counterpoint to Amos 9:7–10, where God's election of other nations is proclaimed to show that Israel will not be exempt from judgment. Divine loyalty, which for Israel always carried connotations of special relationship, is suddenly exploded to new dimensions. Special relationship need not mean exclusive relationship. Even those not in covenant may turn and be saved. The Book of Jonah invites an exclusivistic community to learn lessons in forgiveness of enemies from such a testimony to the abundance of God's loyalty. More than that, reflection on its own history of forgiveness springing from Yahweh's abundant loyalty should guide Israel out of any exclusivism based on self-righteousness. By such indirection, the Jonah story is also testimony to the unswerving faithfulness of God to Israel, not only to other nations.

Second, the Jonah story lifts up what is also emphasized in the full liturgical tradition of Exodus 33: divine loyalty is never to be confused with cheap grace. The forgiveness of the Ninevites is not casual; it is not given without their becoming aware of their status before God as a wicked city. The king and subjects do not assume that divine wrath will be averted; they take what measures of repentance they can, and they hope against hope. So too the Exodus liturgy portrays Yahweh as One who never takes sin lightly, who does mete out judgment. God is indeed patient and forgiving, but that is not the only word. Divine loyalty can never be taken for granted, even though it is abounding. Precisely because Israel has experienced Yahweh's deliverance and Yahweh's theophany and has received the Commandments, this elect people is held accountable in a heightened way.

Within the context of the Mosaic covenantal relationship, God is committed to protect Israel, but not "no matter what." As the party of power in the relationship, the divine suzerain remains ever free to make a new decision, to renew commitment and covenant or to abandon or annihilate the people. Within this theological framework, stories of judgment stand alongside stories of forgiveness. Past instances of forgiveness provide a ground for hope but never a ground for total assurance.

In the third place, therefore, we learn from this tradition of God's *surprising* faithfulness. God's loyalty to Nineveh was scarcely to be counted upon; the Ninevites hoped for it, while Jonah feared it. Israel's situation at Sinai in the aftermath of the golden calf was even more desperate, for the covenant stipulations were clear, the disobedience blatant, and the potential consequences known. Exodus 32 does not focus upon the repentance of the people, because the narrator's purpose is to highlight the effectiveness of Moses as intercessor for them. But the Mosaic covenant context makes clear how great a challenge Moses faced. Disobedience meant end of covenant. Yet divine loyalty overcame even this obstacle. But such exercise of loyalty within this theological framework had to be viewed as ever a surprise, ever a drawing back on God's part from the expected ending of the covenant.

The picture in Jeremiah 16 of the whole people gone astray fits together with the golden calf story of the whole people in rebellion against God. The Sinai covenant is made with Israel as a people. Within limits there may be forgiveness of or judgment upon individuals within the community, but the primary focus is upon God's relationship to the people as a whole, as a people. Thus God's forgiveness consists finally in not abrogating the covenant itself, more than in individual instances of pardon. And that corporate forgiveness, however many times received, could in principle one day not be renewed. God's words to Jeremiah about the removal of loyalty epitomize this possibility. This same possibility of end of covenant is implicit in many other prophetic oracles, such as the chilling lines of Amos 3:2:

> You only have I known
>   of all the families of the earth;
>   therefore I will punish you
>   for all your iniquities.

This lack of certainty about the people's future before God certainly made the divine demand for righteousness and the importance of obedience sharply clear. But it did not say everything Israel wanted to say about divine loyalty. In this Mosaic perspective, divine commitment was understood, but it was subordinated to the freedom of God. The Davidic covenant tradition offered the counterbalance to this Mosaic perspective.

## THE DAVIDIC COVENANT TRADITION: COMMITMENT

It should be said at the outset that the Davidic covenant theology was not developed primarily to handle the theological "weakness" of the Mosaic covenant perspective on loyalty. But insofar as the Davidic tradition emerged in an era of Israel's search for social stability (in both the best and the worst senses of such stability), it provided an alternative which focused on the *promise* of God's supporting presence in the community of faith, no matter what. This alternative has its own "weakness" built in, in that it may emphasize God's obligation to the detriment of divine freedom. But in tandem with the Mosaic perspective, it enhances our understanding of what Yahweh's loyalty to the covenant people is really like.

In the earliest days of Israel's life in the land, its organization was basically tribal. However the various tribes may have come together, the worship of Yahweh and the rejection of Egyptian pharaonic and Canaanite city-state models of political organization were a basic part of what it meant to be "Israel" in those earliest years.[22]

But in the face of increasing pressure from the Philistines, Israel began to move toward a different, more centralized and consolidated form of government—a monarchical state. The Books of Samuel make clear, even through layers of later editing, that the introduction of kingship was a disputed matter. Some parts of the tradition, notably 1 Samuel 8, portray Yahweh as opposed to the change, granting it only as a concession to the people and warning of the dangers of kingship to the life of the common folk. Other material presents kingship as God's own plan to aid Israel (e.g., 1 Sam. 9:16).[23]

Yet even among those who supported kingship and sought to defend it theologically over the centuries of Judah's existence there was not unanimity. The portrayal of the Davidic covenant tradition in Psalm 89 is not fully consistent with that of Psalm 132 or of 2 Samuel 7. The divergence comes precisely in the matter of how to balance God's commitment with God's freedom—the two poles of the concept of loyalty.

Before we turn to Psalm 89 and 2 Samuel 7, it will be useful to mention an ancient Near Eastern political form that appears to have been employed in Israel's interpretation of kingship in Jerusalem. Just as the suzerain-vassal treaty relationship informed the

Mosaic covenant model, so a "royal grant" relationship probably lies behind the Davidic covenant tradition.[24] Royal grants were offered in perpetuity and without condition to servants who had offered faithful service to their rulers; these grants featured land and the role of descendants in control of the land, with the promise that royal favor would not turn aside from the recipient or his descendants. God's irrevocable commitment to the line of Davidic rulers is understood on this analogy,[25] and there are linguistic parallels between the biblical materials and some ancient grant documents. In some cases the vocabulary is actually cognate (using the same consonants in the related Semitic languages), but in other instances the parallels reflect only the same semantic range. This lack of full verbal parallels requires caution in any use of the parallels for assessing the nuances of individual Hebrew words. M. Weinfeld's restricting of divine loyalty to the Davidic covenant tradition[26] seems to me to stem from a too narrow dependence upon general extrabiblical parallels which undermines attention to usage in the biblical tradition itself. The biblical tradition, as I have tried to show, does incorporate loyalty as a theological category within the Mosaic covenant tradition as well.

## Psalm 89

There is no question that the conception of loyalty is of critical importance for Davidic theology. The *locus classicus* for exposition of that covenant tradition is Psalm 89. The poem is far too long (fifty-one verses[27]) to print here in its entirety, but the reader is especially urged to read the full text rather than just the isolated verses quoted. In this psalm the word "loyalty" (RSV "steadfast love") appears some seven times. The word "faithfulness" occurs eight times, six of them in conjunction with loyalty. Covenant with David is mentioned three times, twice in explicit conjunction with loyalty and faithfulness.

The structure and unity of the psalm have been debated, but Artur Weiser's approach seems sensible for the text as handed down to us. Verses 1–18 function as a hymn of praise, with special focus on the Davidic covenant; vv. 19–37 recapitulate the Davidic theme in greater detail, with the motif of the promise set in contrast to the concluding lament (vv. 38–51) over the dire distress of king and people.[28]

Verse 1 opens with praise of Yahweh's loyalty and faithfulness. Verse 2 states the reason they are to be praised: because they are firm and enduring, because loyalty was established in perpetuity. Then vv. 3–4 describe the context in which that enduring loyalty has been made known:

> Thou hast said, "I have made a covenant with my chosen one,
>   I have sworn to David my servant:
> 'I will establish your descendants for ever
>   and build your throne for all generations.' "

The form of these first four verses does not make absolutely clear whether loyalty is the presupposition of the covenant (so Kellenberger), or is to be in effect equated with the covenant (so Weinfeld), or is to be understood as offered to the king within the covenant in the form of its perpetual maintenance. Kellenberger's approach might seem the most straightforward in the particular instance, reading vv. 3–4 as illustration of the results of Yahweh's loyalty. Weinfeld's emphasis can be sustained by the paired usage of "covenant and loyalty" in hendiadys in other passages.[29] The third option is well supported by the evidence of the present study that loyalty occurs essentially within relationship; the emphasis on relationship as context is borne out by the development of the covenant theme in the second part of the psalm, especially vv. 28 and 33–34.

In this case, however, we may do disservice to the richness of the psalm by trying to argue exclusively for any of these three interpretive options at the expense of the others. Indeed, the poem continues with praise to the incomparable God, mighty in battle, creator of the universe, whose heavenly throne is founded on justice and righteousness, before whom stand loyalty and faithfulness. Within this larger context of God's loyalty made known even in the defeat of chaos and maintaining of world order (cf. Ps. 136:4–9), the establishment by covenant of the Davidic line may be viewed as loyalty for Israel and even for the world. In this sense divine loyalty is presupposition of the covenant, as Kellenberger suggests. The king was understood in royal theology to be a "channel of blessing" through whom God established justice, peace, fertility of crops, and longevity among the people (cf. Psalm 72). And in the theological interconnecting of the Davidic and Abrahamic traditions, David's kingdom is viewed as one level of fulfillment of the divine promise of blessing to the nations.[30]

Furthermore, since the focus of Psalm 89 is especially on covenant, it is appropriate also to recognize with Weinfeld the synonymous character of phrases such as "keeping loyalty" (v. 28) and "not violating covenant" (v. 34), of "establishing loyalty" (v. 2) and "making the covenant" (v. 3), of "swearing loyalty" (v. 49) and the "covenant standing firm" (v. 28).

Nonetheless, the middle portion of the psalm makes quite clear that loyalty at the same time is that attribute of God, that attitude and action of God, which typifies life within the covenant, which sustains the Davidides upon the throne. Because Yahweh's "faithfulness and loyalty" will be with the king, all enemies will be defeated (vv. 22–24). The covenant will stand firm because loyalty is kept for him (v. 28).

Verses 30–37 are the strongest Old Testament statement of the unconditional character of this covenant:

> If his children forsake my law
>
> . . . . . . . . . . . .
>
> then I will punish their transgression with the rod
>     and their iniquity with scourges;
> but I will not remove from him my loyalty,
>     or be false to my faithfulness.
> I will not violate my covenant,
>     or alter the word that went forth from my lips.
> Once for all I have sworn by my holiness;
>     I will not lie to David.
> His line shall endure for ever,
>     his throne as long as the sun before me.

Here loyalty is clearly equated with the maintaining of the Davidic line upon the throne, and it is not dependent upon the behavior of the recipients. There will be chastisement, but the relationship between God and the line of David will not come to an end. The grant is made in perpetuity and will never be revoked.

Naturally such a perspective on God's intention was a powerful political tool in the hands of royal propagandists in Jerusalem. The value of such a belief for stable succession and maintaining of control by those in power cannot be underestimated. But this covenant promise serves an important and positive theological function as well. From this perspective the uncertainty of God's presence and forgiveness which characterized the Sinai tradition is overcome by assurance of God's new and deeper commitment to the people through the figure of the king, who mediates God's blessings to them and who symbolically carries their distresses and petitions before Yahweh of hosts, the creator of the universe. Now Yahweh's loyalty to the king, and through the ruler to the people, is no longer surprising; it is promised.

But the third part of Psalm 89 must not go unnoticed. It consists of a bitter and angry complaint against Yahweh because the king has suffered military defeat. The speaker even goes so far as to accuse God:

> Thou hast renounced the covenant with thy servant;
>  thou hast defiled his crown in the dust.
>
> (Ps. 89:39)

And the prayer concludes not with any note of hope but with an agonizing cry:

> Lord, where is thy loyalty of old,
>  which by thy faithfulness thou didst swear to David?
> Remember, O Lord, how thy servant is scorned.
>
> (Ps. 89:49–50a)

This part of the psalm certainly displays the forthrightness, even boldness, of the petitioner. Its importance lies in its indication that the line between "rod and scourges" and "removal of loyalty" was not always clear from a human point of view. And the question of that distinction would become acute in the context of the exile (to be discussed at the conclusion of this chapter).

This discussion of Psalm 89 should not conclude without our considering the significance of the paired terms "loyalty and faithfulness," which appear together either in formal conjunction or in poetic parallelism no fewer than six times in this psalm, as well as in many other theological texts, particularly in the Psalter. The pair has been encountered already in the liturgical proclamation of God's name in Exodus 33. It was suggested in chapter 2, "Stories of Human Loyalty,"[31] that this pair exemplifies hendiadys, with a nuance of constancy being added to emphasize the basic sense of loyalty itself. The psalm texts illustrate a second and complementary way in which the terms can be paired, namely, in poetic parallelism. Just as the word order of the pair always remains constant when the terms are joined by the conjunction "and," so the order is kept consistently in poetic usage. "Loyalty" occurs in the first line, "faithfulness" in the second line of the pair. Here in Psalm 89, as in the secular texts examined earlier, we find the word pair emphasized in connection with an oath taken by the one who is to act loyally. Here, however, the oath is not requested by the recipient of loyalty as a means of attaining certainty of the outcome. Rather, the oath is probably understood as part of the covenant process on the analogy of the royal grant. The offering of the oath serves as God's assurance to the Davidic line of the maintaining of the commitment undertaken. So here also, "faithfulness" serves to underline the conception of loyalty as an attitude that will hold fast over time, an attitude that will never fade or waver and that can thus be counted upon to issue in supportive action on any occasion of distress. The king's cry at the end of Psalm 89 that *loyalty sworn* by *faithfulness* seems nowhere to be found brings the three terms together in a climax of protest and poignant bewilderment. It is indeed as if the impossible has happened; the one sure thing in all of life seems to have been swept away. But although God's way is incomprehensible to the petitioner, the cry still goes up to God. The turn of events did not lead to disbelief. The question is still put to God, "Where is thy loyalty?"

Although the combination of the terms "loyalty" and "faithfulness" is here tied explicitly to a covenant context, the terms also come together in psalms that contain no special covenantal focus. Kellenberger notes this point and in this context objects to the translation "covenant loyalty" for the single word "loyalty."[32] He is correct that such texts are silent on the matter of covenant. While it is best, as he suggests, not to import covenant as an overt reference everywhere loyalty is mentioned, it is still the case that one or another or a combination of the major covenant conceptions undergirded much of ancient Israel's corporate and individual world view and was presupposed in its liturgical life.

Psalms 36 and 57, for example, as prayers for deliverance each incorporate the general statement:

> For thy loyalty is great to the heavens,
> thy faithfulness to the clouds.
> (Ps. 57:10; cf. Ps. 36:5)

No special covenant focus is evident in the immediate context. But the individual Israelite's theological identity came from being part of the covenant community to which Yahweh had been revealed at Sinai and for which Yahweh had established kingship as governance. This underlying world view can be functioning without being explicitly expressed.

Psalm 98 raises this theme in the setting of a hymn about the kingship of Yahweh. Such psalms have often been held to have been used in connection with covenant renewal liturgies in Jerusalem.[33] But even if they were used more generally, the expression would surely call to mind covenant as the framework of Yahweh's care for Israel:

> He has remembered his loyalty and faithfulness
> to the house of Israel.
> All the ends of the earth have seen
> the victory of our God.
> (Ps. 98:3)

The emphasis on constancy or reliability in interpreting this word pair should be supplemented by the observation that the connotation of truth remains also a part of the term "faithfulness." "Truth" is a traditional older English translation for the Hebrew term. The proclamation that God's "truth endures to all generations" (Ps. 100:5b) carries overtones for modern English speakers which are too abstract to be appropriate to the Hebrew, so the translation "faithfulness" is preferable. But the idea that God will carry through on words spoken, so that the covenant promise remains "true," should still be seen as part of the meaning of the line. That sense comes through most explicitly again in Ps. 89:33–34, where the emphasis is that God will not turn back from the sworn oath, with the summation, "I will not lie to David."

Isaiah 40:8 states the theme well:

> The grass withers, the flower fades;
> but the word of our God will stand for ever.

The previous verses of this Isaiah passage compare "all flesh" to the grass which withers. There is a textual problem, but it is possible that human loyalty (rather than RSV's beauty) is compared to the flower of the field. The permanence of God's intention as contrasted to human intentions is clearly in view. God's word will stand.

In sum, faithfulness encompasses both the reliability of God as constancy over time and the assurance that divine promises will be kept. For those who know their very existence to be in dependence upon the loyalty of Yahweh, this strengthening of loyalty to "faithful loyalty" or "sure loyalty" gives heightened expression to the trustworthiness of the benevolent and saving God. Little wonder, then, that the paired terms "loyalty" and "faithfulness" are found in prayers of petition, thanksgiving, and praise, as well as in explicitly covenantal contexts. Earthly support may fail, and God's ways may be inscrutable, but the last word, and the first, for Israel is:

> For the Lord is good;
> his loyalty endures for ever,
> and his faithfulness to all generations.
> (Ps. 100:5)

## 2 Samuel 7

The narrative of Yahweh's covenant with David is recorded in 2 Samuel 7. Clearly there is interplay in the tradition between this text and Psalm 89, but there are special nuances in the Deuteronomic historian's handling of this covenant tradition.[34] In this key passage, the prophet Nathan brings Yahweh's word to David, in response to David's proposal to build a "house" (temple) for

Yahweh. In brief, the reply is that David will not build Yahweh's "house"; rather, Yahweh will build David's "house" (dynasty):

> Moreover the Lord declares to you that the Lord will make you a house. . . . I will raise up your offspring after you . . . , and I will establish his kingdom. He shall build a house for my name, and I will establish the throne of his kingdom for ever. . . . When he commits iniquity, I will chasten him with the rod of men, with the stripes of the sons of men; but I will not take my loyalty from him, as I took it from Saul, whom I put away from before you. And your house and your kingdom shall be made sure for ever before me; your throne shall be established for ever. (2 Sam. 7:11b–16)

Here, as in Psalm 89, the nature of the covenant with David is stated unconditionally. The dynasty will enjoy God's loyalty forever, and any sin will be punished by human hand but not by the final judgment of the removal of divine loyalty.[35] The contrast with Saul looks back to the tradition which records two versions of the sin for which God rejected him. First Sam. 13:7b–15 attributes Saul's loss of dynastic right to a misappropriation of priestly functions, and 1 Samuel 15 focuses on his taking of booty rather than destroying everything after the victory over Amalek. In their present form, these traditions emphasize the importance attached to obeying God's word and the power of the prophet over the king. While the age of the stories is not certain, some such theme would probably have developed early on among Jerusalem theologians as a companion piece to the Davidic covenant, to explain why the line of Israel's second king was to continue in contrast to that of the first. The tensions between the Saulides and the Davidides were long-lived, and such an explanation would have been needed.

Theologically, the contrast between David and Saul draws indirect attention to the contrast between the Davidic and Mosaic traditions. What happened to Saul can be viewed as the potential consequence of applying the theology of the Sinai covenant to the context of kingship. The disobedient one is removed from leadership; except for God's willingness to raise up a new leader, the end of Israel before God would be in view. In fact, it appears likely (to the extent that we can trust the prophetic accounts of 1—2 Kings historiographically) that in the northern part of the divided kingdom the kind of theology associated with Saul's rejection continued to operate. Dynasties came and went, and several times the narrator relates a prophet's role in proclaiming (like Samuel) the end of one line and the inauguration of another.[36]

The Davidic theology overcomes such political and theological uncertainty in its declaration of the new state of affairs which pertains to David's line. In 2 Samuel 7, as in Psalm 89, loyalty takes shape in all the care of God which will maintain the Davidic throne; removing of loyalty would be tantamount to the ending of the covenant. The promise is simply, magnificently, that Yahweh's faithfulness will stand sure no matter what.

It is a matter of dispute whether this dramatically unconditional Davidic covenant perspective emerged very early and was later modified in the face of the disaster attendant upon the exile, or whether the earliest perspective was conditional and only gradually was developed into the completely unconditional view that we find in 2 Samuel 7 and Psalm 89. Psalm 132 makes clear that there was some changing of perspective over a period of time. Here the divine oath to David contains a clearly conditional statement:

> If your sons keep my covenant
>   and my testimonies which I shall teach them,
> their sons also for ever
>   shall sit upon your throne.
>
> (Ps. 132:12)

We cannot know finally whether this psalm is early, late, or revised in the light of events. It would be plausible to suppose that the unconditional motif emerged under Solomon, with a less absolute viewpoint being held in the early years of David's rule. But naturally the collapse of the monarchy would bring about theological reassessment as well.

The historian himself saw the prime example of human punishment of the Davidic line in the stripping away of the northern ("Israelite") tribes from Jerusalem's rule following the death of Solomon. The word "Israel" in 1 Kings 2:4; 8:25; and 9:4–5 refers explicitly to the Northern Kingdom and thus these passages are to be taken, not as modifications of 2 Samuel 7 toward a conditional viewpoint, but rather as confirmation of its promise.[37]

Yet even as these passages confirm the promise, the historian appears to have walked a tightrope between the Davidic and Sinai traditions in a different way. In contrast to Psalm 89, the actual word "covenant" is conspicuous by its absence in 2 Samuel 7. In fact, the term "covenant" seems to have only rare and restricted theological use in the Deuteronomic history. The phrase "covenant and loyalty" found in Deut. 7:9, 12 (part of the historian's theological sourcebook) appears in an explicitly conditional context and in application to the whole community, despite allusions to the patriarchs. And although the term "loyalty" is used in the history with reference to the Davidic tradition, the word "covenant" is restricted to occasions in which we find reference to the whole people and the law, not just reference to the royal line.[38] Thus in its own way the Deuteronomic history seeks to weave together the royal theology's emphasis on God's promised faithfulness with the old Mosaic theology of surprising faithfulness.

The tension and balance between the two covenant traditions would give an important word to the people of Josiah's era—a word of comfort and of challenge. The promise to David serves to explain for the late preexilic community how it is that the kingdom has persisted, despite its apostasy which seemed to the historian quite analogous to that of the now defunct Northern Kingdom. This explanation serves as comfort in that there is sure hope for the people because of God's commitment to them. At the same time, the story of Solomon and Rehoboam and the restricted use of the word "covenant" serve as reminder to king and people that God's gracious faithfulness ought never to be taken for granted. The human punishment which came upon the Davidic line—loss of the north—was no light judgment; it had diplomatic consequences for centuries, even to Josiah's time, a century after the fall of Samaria. Thus the challenge to obedience sounds forth to the whole community. Covenant is not a matter of promise to the king, but of command to all the community. God's forbearance should become the occasion for repentance, recommitment, and rejoicing, not for business as usual.

EXILIC DEVELOPMENTS:
GOD'S NEW WAY

With the fall of Jerusalem in 587 B.C. the understanding of loyalty in each of these covenant traditions was brought into radical question. The notion of God's promised loyalty to the line of David lay in shambles with the deportation of Jehoiachin and Zedekiah. The razing of the temple and the destruction of the city of Jerusalem served only to underline the disaster that had come upon the royal family, since the enduring nature of Zion and David had been theologically so closely linked. If God's loyalty was not sure after all, then the very existence (or power) of Yahweh had to be called into question.

By the same token, the exile meant radical dislocation for those imbued with the old Mosaic covenant emphases. Loss of the land was the final symbol of rejection by Yahweh for disobedience. So long as God's surprising faithfulness had prevailed, the covenant could continue to function theologically. But with the realization of its most radical threat, the basis for identity as a people was washed away. If God had rejected the community, then it would seem that the people must seek out some other divine protector and begin again.

A variety of theological responses enabled Israel to discover that its relationship with Yahweh was not, after all, at an end.[39] In two of these responses especially, Second Isaiah and the Priestly writer, the theme of loyalty was reinterpreted as a basis for understanding God's new way with the community devoid of land and king. Each brought God's loyalty into new focus as old traditions of faith were sifted and reapplied to address the situation in Babylon.

## Second Isaiah

Many people find the poetry of Isaiah 40—55 the most stirring of all in the Old Testament. The scope of the work, ranging from creation to new creation, and its concern for the place of all nations and peoples within that creation have drawn readers to it generation after generation. Within this wide-sweeping setting, Yahweh's ongoing intention for Israel is proclaimed.

Second Isaiah has a great deal to say about the future of Zion (Jerusalem). Yet he shows no interest in the renewal of the Davidic monarchy. This use of Zion without David is truly remarkable, since throughout the royal theological tradition the two were intimately bound together. In the same way, this prophet splits apart the two key aspects of the Mosaic covenant tradition. On the one hand, he has a great deal to say about the exodus theme; the imagery of the exodus from Egypt is basic to his picture of the return from Babylon to Zion, portrayed under the figure of a new exodus. Yet on the other hand, there is no reference whatsoever to Sinai or to the covenant associated with Moses. There are references to Israel's sin and to Yahweh's mercy, but they are never developed in the language of that conditional covenant. It is as if the prophet has seen to the heart of the bankruptcy of each of the two main theological streams to which the community was heir. In the reworking of selected portions of Israel's theological resources a new word of Yahweh breaks into the exilic situation.[40]

The prophet turns twice explicitly to the concept of loyalty, in 55:3b–5 and in 54:7–10. These two texts epitomize in brief compass the ways in which the prophet transformed the David and Sinai portions of the classic covenant traditions. These brief allusions to a radically transformed perspective on loyalty serve as clue to and confirmation of the larger picture of Zion without David and exodus without Sinai, which can be seen in the corpus as a whole.

Isaiah 55:3b–5 contains the one explicit reference to David in Second Isaiah,[41] and it is joined together with the words "covenant" and "loyalty." Yet the proclamation given does not promise the restoration of the Davidic line. Rather, the Davidic promise and vocation are transferred:

> And I will make with you an everlasting covenant,
>     my trustworthy loyalty for David.
> Behold, I made him a witness to the peoples,
>     a leader and commander for the peoples.
> Behold, you shall call nations that you know not,
>     and nations that knew you not shall run to you,

> because of the Lord your God, and of the Holy One of Israel,
> for he has glorified you.
>
> (Isa. 55:3b–5)

This text forms part of the dramatic conclusion to this portion of the Book of Isaiah. In these lines the prophet announces that God's relationship to David is to be "democratized" to become the promised foundation of the people directly, not through the royal line. Correspondingly, the Davidic vocation to be a blessing to the nations is also "democratized" and becomes the true calling of the whole people.[42] This proclamation offers, as it were, the prophet's response to the bitter lament which concludes Psalm 89 with its cry, "Where is thy loyalty?" The prophet's words incorporate also verbal allusions to Psalm 18, a royal thanksgiving psalm in which the Davidic king's role as "head of the nations" (Ps. 18:43) is developed. In this passage, as elsewhere in the Davidic tradition, the words "covenant" and "loyalty" become nearly synonymous.[43] In highly elliptical poetic style the prophet makes loyalty a second object of the verb for covenant making, and the "everlasting" character of the covenant with the people is explicitly stated in a manner reminiscent of the Abrahamic covenant in the exilic Priestly work (Gen. 17:13). It should be noted that the precise expression "everlasting covenant" is not used of the royal covenant with David in Old Testament tradition, despite the fact that the perpetual character of that covenant is so much emphasized in terms of its irrevocability. The expression used here is instead typical of various exilic forms of a covenant with all the people (Gen. 17:13; Jer. 32:40; Ezek. 16:60; 37:26). Thus the very wording of Isa. 55:3b–5 points to the theological reinterpretation in which the recipient of Yahweh's loyalty is changed from the Jerusalem dynasty to the community as a whole. This community, then, as recipient of divine loyalty, will serve as blessing to the nations.

The question whether Israel's role vis-à-vis the nations is to be active or passive has been long discussed. Despite the verb "to summon" used here, the conclusion of the passage in v. 5b seems to support a passive role for Israel. The nations will turn to Yahweh because of what Yahweh has done for Israel, not because of any action by Israel. God's preserving of the people and returning them to Zion will be a "new thing" even greater than the preservation of the Davidic line in the past. The very existence of the people will stand as witness to the nations of the power and loyal care of Yahweh.

This democratization of the Davidic covenant and vocation is set in the context of the great invitation to all who hunger and thirst to attend a great banquet, free of charge:

> Ho, every one who thirsts,
> come to the waters.
> (Isa. 55:1)

The call goes out to the community in exile to receive the good news of the new and deeper meaning of that old covenant with David. Those who have given up on Yahweh because of their too small picture of the ways of God with the people are invited to "hear, that your soul may live" (v. 3a). To the skeptic who supposes that this transformation is only a salvage operation by a desperate but unrealistic theologian, Yahweh says:

> My thoughts are not your thoughts,
> neither are your ways my ways.
> (Isa. 55:8)

The creator of all, before whom the nations are as a drop in a bucket (40:15), can indeed transform an old promise into a new and greater one, one that encompasses and gives new depth to the old. God's loyalty to the community will no longer be experienced through the king as channel of blessing. Rather, as in the heritage of Abraham and Sarah (51:2), divine loyalty will be directly known, not tied to the vicissitudes of any particular earthly form of government.

The term "loyalty" also occasions Second Isaiah's reinterpretation of the Sinai tradition. The term "covenant" does not appear, but the imagery in the key passage is that of a marriage broken but now to be restored. The words are addressed to Zion:

> For your Maker is your husband,
> . . . . . . . . . . . . . .
> For the Lord has called you
> like a wife forsaken and grieved in spirit,

like a wife of youth when she is cast off,
  says your God.
For a brief moment I forsook you,
  but with great compassion I will gather you.
In overflowing wrath for a moment
  I hid my face from you,
but with everlasting loyalty I will have compassion on you,
  says the Lord, your Redeemer.

(Isa. 54:5–8)

The marriage relationship as metaphor for God's relationship with Israel is not new with Second Isaiah. It is a dominant motif in the opening chapters of Hosea and is used also in Jeremiah 2—3 and in Ezekiel 16 and 23. In all of these the emphasis is on the infidelity of the wife, and in each case the metaphor is used to represent the Sinai covenant relationship between Yahweh and Israel. I find myself among many women and men who today find the one-sidedness of this marriage imagery difficult to deal with.[44] In its ancient context, nonetheless, the metaphor is employed to emphasize the intimacy and caring aspect of the relationship between Yahweh and Israel which is implicit but not self-evident within the more basic political metaphor of suzerain and vassal. The hurt of God, who is rejected despite all the gifts lavished upon Israel, the foolishness of Israel, and the rejection of the rejected all come through in this tradition.[45] Only Hosea of these three earlier prophets makes explicit use of the marriage image in his new covenant material; although he describes the restored covenant relationship as everlasting (Hos. 2:19a), the place of divine loyalty within it is not mentioned.[46]

Here in Isaiah 54 the prophet reworks this marriage metaphor from earlier prophecy. The emphasis, as is typical of Second Isaiah, is on restoration rather than on the sin of the people. Yet their guilt is implied in the reference to Yahweh's wrath. God did not turn away from the people without reason. But now it is the *everlasting* loyalty of God the divine husband which is the basis for breaking out of the pattern of requiting of iniquity in the Sinai tradition. Although that covenant is not mentioned, the tradition of marriage imagery suggests that Sinai is in the background. The renewal of the marriage, the overflow of compassion, stems from a depth of commitment which cannot be confined to the bounds of the warnings built into the Decalogue. Here the restoration is not even predicated upon repentance, but only upon the loyalty of God—which in this context must be regarded as the most marvelously and fundamentally surprising loyalty imaginable. The "terms" of the Sinai covenant relationship are undone. The surprising faithfulness, offered here in the greatest surprise of all, is transformed into promised faithfulness for all time to come.

> For as the heavens are higher than the earth,
>  so are my ways higher than your ways
>  and my thoughts than your thoughts.
> (Isa. 55:9)

All the proclamation of restoration to Zion is conceivable only when it is grounded in this new word of divine loyalty.

That theme is made even more clear in the next strophe of Isaiah 54:

> For this is like the days of Noah to me:
>  as I swore that the waters of Noah
>  should no more go over the earth,
> so I have sworn that I will not be angry with you
>  and will not rebuke you.
> For the mountains may depart
>  and the hills be removed,
> but my loyalty shall not depart from you,
>  and my covenant of peace shall not be removed,
>  says the Lord, who has compassion on you.
> (Isa. 54:9–10)

The poet relates the new promise to Zion to the first of the great covenants of ancient times, to one made on behalf of all peoples, not only Israel. Just as in the aftermath of the destruction of creation in the time of Noah God promised, "Never again," so now to the chosen people comes the promise of "Never again," of a permanent future based on the sure ground of divine loyalty. The covenant of peace[47] will supplant the Sinai covenant. Its permanence, sure as the very existence of the mountains and hills, is described in a way reminiscent of the promise of the people's future in Jer. 31:35–37, where comparison to the fixed order of creation follows upon the proclamation of a new covenant. The power of God to redeem and the willingness of God to forgive are bound up in the single image of the steadfastness of creation itself. Yahweh's loyalty in the end overcomes any obstacle. God, whose ways are not like human ways, who is free to let go of Israel and start again, has not and will not let go. Here is the quintessential exercise of loyalty. The One who is forever free chooses to remain bound to this weak and needy people, that they may bear witness before all nations that Yahweh alone is God.

*Other Exilic Prophecy*

References to divine loyalty in other prophetic material are sparsely scattered, but most of them ring consistent with Second Isaiah's emphasis on the power of God's loyalty to outlast the failings of the people.[48] The theme comes up twice, for instance, in Jeremiah, in 31:3 and 3:12 (where RSV "merciful" is better translated "the loyal One"). Both of these texts seem to have been originally related to Jeremiah's appeal to the people of the old (defunct) Northern Kingdom to join in Yahweh worship in Jerusalem, but both (especially chap. 31) seem to have been later reinterpreted to apply to the people of Judah in exile as well. Each proclaims a forgiveness which goes beyond what the people have a right to expect under the terms of the Mosaic covenant. Loyalty that is prolonged overcomes anger and invites the people into a future of rejoicing in the presence of Yahweh. The door is not closed. All that is required is a "yes" of repentance to the invitation offered.

So also in Mic. 7:18–20, loyalty is intimately associated with forgiveness. These verses are part of a section usually regarded as an exilic or postexilic supplement to the core of Micah. Here it is the promise to the patriarchs which provides the ground for loyalty going beyond the conditional character of Sinai, just as the patriarchs provided the ground for Second Isaiah to move beyond the Davidic promise:

> He does not retain his anger for ever
> because he delights in loyalty.

> He will again have compassion upon us,
>> he will tread our iniquities under foot.
> Thou wilt cast all our sins
>> into the depths of the sea.
> Thou wilt show faithfulness to Jacob
>> and loyalty to Abraham,
> as thou hast sworn to our fathers
>> from the days of old.
>
> (Mic. 7:18b–20)

In its own way, the Micah text plays on the Exodus 34 liturgical expression of forgiving loyalty in the Mosaic covenant. In Exodus 34, God is slow to anger, but in Micah 7 God does not remain angry. In Exodus 34, God forgives but yet punishes; in Micah, God forgives, even to the point of obliterating all the people's sins. Loyalty here is manifest first of all in forgiveness, and only then in the persistent maintaining of the relationship into the future.

The emphasis on forgiveness in the prophetic conception of loyalty may give the impression that loyalty here is really synonymous with "grace" or "mercy." Despite this surface appearance, it is probable that the nuancing is more subtle. Hebrew does have other words for grace *(ḥēn)* and mercy *(raḥămîm)*, which occasionally appear along with loyalty in these passages. The nuance of the word "loyalty" remains that paradoxical combination of freedom and commitment; loyalty is the basis out of which Yahweh extends grace, mercy, forgiveness to the community. Because of their sin the people are not "deserving" of God's grace; yet one can say they *are* "deserving," simply because they are in relationship with God. The reality of that relationship is a given, and Yahweh chooses to honor that commitment. Part of the power of the marriage metaphor lies in its capacity to convey the notion of a relationship never really undone, despite even the formalities of a divorce declaration.[49] Likewise the appeal to the patriarchal tradition implies that Yahweh's commitment and free decision are the basic categories for loyalty. In Abraham the commitment is given deeper rootage than that provided by the Sinai tradition alone.

## The Priestly Writer

In the Priestly work, the theological resource of the Abrahamic covenant is systematically developed. P's interest in Sinai is focused, not upon covenant or stipulations, but rather upon the gift of the cult (its rituals, leaders, and material equipment) whereby the relationship between Yahweh and people which was initiated with Abraham can be brought to culmination, so that Yahweh can truly be present in the midst of the people.

But surprisingly, loyalty is not a dominant category in Priestly theology. In fact, the word is scarcely mentioned at all in his own writing. Whether this silence is a matter of chance or of active disinterest we cannot know. It might be said that P tends to "ignore" both the Mosaic and the Davidic covenant traditions in the sense that there is no specific play upon them in the text.[50] The "eternal covenant" with Abraham does not make explicit mention of loyalty. At the same time, the purpose of this exilic work was surely, like that of Second Isaiah, to provide a new theological grounding for Israel's faith.

While old theological themes are not explicitly reused, the incorporation of Old Epic (JE) material into the scope of the Priestly work offers some indications of how such traditional themes were transformed in the process of receiving a new setting.[51] The story of the spies in Numbers 13—14 can be viewed in this way. N. Lohfink has called this incident the second of Israel's three "original" sins in the Priestly narrative's perspective;[52] thus it is a critical passage for understanding P's view of divine response to a disobedient people. The narrative offers a fitting conclusion to the entire discussion of loyalty in covenant tradition, for it incorporates and transforms material composed from a Mosaic covenant perspective.

In the received form of this Numbers 13—14 tradition, which is largely from the hand of P, Moses sends twelve spies (one from each tribe) to reconnoiter the land. On their return they report its wonderful fertility, but add that it is impossible to occupy because of the strength of its inhabitants. Only Caleb and Joshua among the twelve dissent from this defeatist opinion. The people follow the majority and propose to choose a new leader and return to Egypt. Thereupon Yahweh announces that the people will be disinherited; but Moses' powerful intercession turns the judgment aside. The present generation will die in the wilderness, but Caleb, Joshua, and the second generation will eventually enter the land. Although the text has been thoroughly reworked, so that absolute source-critical certainty cannot be attained,[53] it does seem clear that earlier stages of the story presented two other conclusions: (1) no one except Caleb would enter the land (Num. 14:23b–24, Old Epic) and (2) no one of "this people" would enter, but a new line would begin from Moses (14:11b–23a, pre-P supplement to the Old Epic).

Even in the brief fragments of the Old Epic tradition, the gravity of Israel's sin is clearly stated in the verb "to despise," which in Hebrew is not simply emotive but has connotations of total rejection of the covenant relationship. Hebrew usage also suggests that the sin of despising cannot go unpunished, even if repentance should later occur. Here in the context of the Mosaic covenant tradition, we see Israel's rejection of the suzerain, and the covenant is made concrete in their desire to replace Yahweh's chosen leader Moses and in their plan to return to Egypt. At the very point of achieving the goal of their deliverance they propose to return to bondage.

Numbers 14:11b–23a form a supplement to the Old Epic material which covers God's response, Moses' intercession, and a portion of the outcome of the story. This supplement, regarded as "deuteronomic," certainly operates within the Mosaic covenant framework when taken on its own. Moses' intercession is obviously intended to relate to the liturgical formulation of the divine name given in Exod. 34:6–7, and is also a refraction of his key intercession in the matter of the golden calf, Exod. 32:11–12. It is here that the concept of loyalty plays a critical role, as Moses cites God's own self-revelation as the ground for his appeal:

> And now, I pray thee, let the power of the Lord be great as thou hast promised, saying, "The Lord is slow to anger, and abounding in loyalty, forgiving iniquity and transgression, but he will by no means clear the guilty. . . ." Pardon the iniquity of this people, I pray thee,

according to the greatness of thy loyalty, and according as thou hast forgiven this people, from Egypt even until now. (Num. 14:17–19)

Just as in the story of the golden calf, so here too disobedience should mean the end of the covenant relationship, the more so because the people themselves have in effect proposed to end it. But Moses makes bold to ask that God's response to the golden calf, God's surprising faithfulness, abounding loyalty, may be made manifest yet one more time. As in the extended liturgical tradition of Exodus 34, the greatness of God's loyalty is counted upon to extend even to forgiveness, the realm where frail human loyalty might fall short. Yahweh's answer comes:

I have pardoned, according to your word; but truly . . . none of the men who have seen my glory and my signs . . . and have not hearkened to my voice, shall see the land. (Num. 14:20–23a)

This response is puzzling at first, since forgiveness and judgment are held together in a single sentence. What can forgiveness possibly mean in such a setting? The real content of forgiveness here is God's decision not to end the covenant relationship, not to disinherit the people and begin over again with Moses. Even though the wilderness generation will wander thirty-eight more years until all of them have died, the covenant community itself and the promise of the land remain intact. Forgiveness does not mean that sin has no consequences, that life goes on as if nothing had happened. Forgiveness means rather that God's loyalty is extended to the community in a way which the people have no right to expect in view of their behavior. Faithfulness overcomes unfaithfulness in the surprising loyalty of God.

What happens when this older witness to God's surprising faithfulness is incorporated into the Priestly narrative? The P tradition focuses its attention more on the punishment meted out to particular individuals (the spies, those age twenty and over) and links this story with others in a sequence of "murmurings" against Yahweh. Since the punishment theme is so expanded, it might seem that the older forgiveness tradition becomes inconsequential or even stands awkwardly as an embarrassment in the final form of the text. But this old tradition still serves to explain how it came about that the covenant people did continue as Yahweh's people. Even though the Priestly presupposition is the permanence of Yahweh's covenant with the people through their ancestor Abraham (Genesis 17), P still must have some ground for dealing with this second "original" sin: at the heart of the Abrahamic covenant is the land promise, and it is just this promise which the people now spurn and mistrust.

By focusing on the distinction between generations, P suggests that Israel in exile should "mimic Joshua's faith and that of the second generation in the wilderness, who walked in perfection and the land was theirs."[54] But if the exiles in Babylon were disparaging the land, as N. Lohfink and Ralph W. Klein suggest, this was surely partly so because they did not think they could ever live in it again, since the exile symbolized that God had rejected them. People often protect themselves by disparaging what is irretrievably lost. To exhort the people to a positive attitude toward the land was therefore not enough. They needed also to be offered a basis for believing that their attitude could still make a difference. And it is just such a basis for hope which the incorporated old tradition offers within the Numbers narrative. Moses' intercession and God's reply, "I have pardoned," make clear that God's loyalty can overcome sin, even the greatest sin. The divine promise to be God to Abraham's descendants is thus stamped "confirmed" by illustration from the wilderness history. The emphasis has shifted in the final framework of the narrative from surprising loyalty to promised loyalty. Yahweh's loyalty is the basis for hope for those in exile.

Neither the tradition that emphasized "surprise" nor that which emphasized "promise" could capture all of what Israel came to know was important about God's loyalty. The Mosaic covenant tradition was able to view sin radically seriously, to insist upon the divine demand for a just and faithful people, but it ran the risk of undercutting the steadfastness of God's care for the community. Even though it extended God's loyalty to include forgiveness, it led to a theology of uncertainty; for despite the long history of God's forbearance, each occasion of disobedience raised anew the possibility that the people might be cast off forever. The royal theology, and the associated patriarchal traditions, solved this problem by emphasizing the permanence of God's covenant. But the move in this direction was open to a different danger, the danger of regarding sin too casually, as the famous "temple sermon" of Jeremiah 7 made clear.

Each of the major covenant traditions thus contributes its own strength to a heritage in which loyalty conveyed both the freedom and the commitment of Yahweh toward a weak and needy people, a loyalty which in the end was seen to transcend every political form and overcome every stumbling block of sin.

## NOTES

1. See also Abraham and Abimelech (Gen. 21:22–34). In some instances the English terms "pact" and "treaty" may be preferred, since in modern English the word "covenant" tends to be used explicitly theologically, while these stories are basically secular.

2. Edgar Kellenberger, *ḥäsäd wä'ᵃmät als Ausdruck einer Glaubenserfahrung*, ANANT 69 (Zurich: Theologischer Verlag, 1982), 50–52. He has more difficulty with the David-Jonathan narrative.

3. See chapter 2, "Stories of Human Loyalty," and especially my *Meaning of Ḥesed*, HSM 17 (Missoula, Mont.: Scholars Press, 1978), 58–78.

4. This example is the strongest of the three Kellenberger uses. Note that it is also much like the Rahab story except for the absence of the word "covenant" in the latter. In both cases, loyalty and creating of relationship are closely tied; but in my view the loyalty is always understood in the context of some level of relationship, rather than shown just in order to create the relationship. The distinction is subtle, but it is important when we come to assess the meaning of Yahweh's covenant loyalty to Israel.

5. Nelson Glueck, *Ḥesed in the Bible* (Cincinnati: Hebrew Union College Press, 1967; German original, Giessen: Töpelmann, 1927), passim.

6. So Félix Asensio, *Misericordia et Veritas, el Ḥesed y 'Emet divinos, su influjo religioso-social en la historia de Israel*, Analecta Gregoriana 48, Sec. 3, no. 19 (Rome: Apud Aedes Universitatis Gregorianae, 1949). This view may be compared to Kellenberger's concern for the strength of loyalty which can overcome even breach of trust.

7. So Sidney Hills in a 1957 unpublished manuscript. For a summary of Hills's work, see my *Meaning of Ḥesed*, 10–12.

8. Kellenberger, *ḥäsäd*, 77, 81.

9. The understanding of covenant forms has evoked a lively contemporary debate. For a convenient summary of issues, positions, and bibliography, see two articles in IDBSup (Nashville: Abingdon Press, 1976): M. Weinfeld's "Covenant, Davidic," 188–92, and P. Riemann's "Covenant, Mosaic," 192–96. As these essays show, there has been considerable refinement over the past three decades in scholarly understanding of treaty analogies from the world of ancient Near Eastern politics and diplomacy. The ongoing discussion focuses especially upon the applicability of these models to the interpretation of specific biblical passages or blocks of material and upon the extent to which the Davidic and Mosaic models functioned as competing or complementary theological perspectives in the history of Israel's traditions. The next sections of this chapter must inevitably make some assumptions about these matters; full debate on all the background issues is not practicable here. It is possible to consider the theological impact of the material even without sure identification of all the tradents and stages of tradition.

10. See, for example, the criticisms of Dennis J. McCarthy, *Old Testament Covenant: A Survey of Current Opinions* (Richmond: John Knox Press, 1972), 13–21, 30–31.

11. It is understood, however, that the suzerain will continue to protect the obedient vassal and will take disciplinary action against the rebellious vassal. Thus the treaty relationships were not quite so one-sided as has sometimes been suggested. For a fuller description of the form of these treaties, see, for example, Delbert R. Hillers, *Covenant: The History of a Biblical Idea* (Baltimore: Johns Hopkins University Press, 1969), chaps. 2–3, pp. 25–71.

12. Although the formal language and vocabulary of blessing and cursing is, of course, not used here, the theme of the two possibilities, the choice between life and death (cf. Deuteronomy 30), is certainly present.

13. McCarthy, *Old Testament Covenant,* 13–21. McCarthy notes such literary differences as sentence structure in the giving of the suzerain's name, brevity of the alleged "historical prologue" phrase, and absence of blessing and curse formulae. Uncertainties about the dating of the biblical material and of Israel's theological adapting of the political metaphor underscore the need for caution in comparative work.

14. The Decalogue is traditionally separable into two "tables" of love of God and love of neighbor. But observing either table apart from the other was not only inadequate from Israel's point of view, it was impossible. Love of neighbor was predicated upon love of God; love of God was mockery and falsehood apart from justice in the community. This theme will be the focus of the discussion of chap. 5, "Loyalty: The Calling of the People of God."

78    *FAITHFULNESS IN ACTION*

15. See William L. Moran, "The Ancient Near Eastern Background of the Love of God in Deuteronomy," *CBQ* 25 (1963):77–87.

16. For a suggestive treatment of how this vision would be perceived differently by "haves" and "have-nots," see Walter Brueggemann, *Living Toward a Vision: Biblical Reflections on Shalom* (Philadelphia: United Church Press, 1976), 27–36.

17. See Brevard Childs, *The Book of Exodus,* OTL (Philadelphia: Westminster Press, 1974), 367.

18. The materials of Exodus 32—34 are extremely complex traditio-historically; such issues will be alluded to only as they impinge directly upon the theological reflection. For concise discussion of these matters, see Childs, *Exodus,* 557–62, 584–86, 604–10; also, R. W. L. Moberly, *At the Mountain of God: Story and Theology in Exodus 32—34* (Sheffield: JSOT Press, 1983).

19. The Hebrew term in each of these expressions is *'ēl,* a relatively rare term for God by comparison to the more usual *'ĕlōhîm.* It is quite possible that the Hebrew should here be rendered El, one of the ancient titles of the God of Israel. In any case, the indefinite article of the RSV and other English translations obscures the titular character of the appellation.

20. Kellenberger (*ḥäsäd,* 81) associates this persistent character of divine loyalty with the term "faithfulness" as well. See below, this chapter, 57–60.

21. The examples given here focus on the community as a whole. Psalms 86 and 103 illustrate this association of forgiveness and loyalty in prayers of individuals. See chap. 4, "Help in Need."

22. The emergence and organization of premonarchic Israel is very much under debate today. Martin Noth's amphictyonic hypothesis has received valid criticism, but no replacement model has yet achieved consensus. N. Gottwald's approach (*The Tribes of Yahweh* [Maryknoll, N.Y.: Orbis Books, 1979]) has evoked a lively discussion of the issues. In any case, the closeness of relationship between groups of tribes located in the northern and southern regions is rightly questioned on the basis of David's two-stage rise to power (2 Sam. 2:4; 5:3). It is not certain to what degree the "all Israel" character of religious festivals such as that described in Joshua 24 has been read back into the era of the judges by the later tradition.

23. The problems of sorting through these materials have been alluded to in chap. 2, "Stories of Human Loyalty," 8, and n. 1. See in addition Baruch Halpern, "The Uneasy Compromise: Israel Between League and Monarchy," in *Traditions in Transformation: Turning Points in Biblical Faith,* eds. Baruch Halpern and Jon D. Levenson (Winona Lake, Ind.: Eisenbrauns, 1981), 64–67.

24. See in particular the work of Weinfeld, summarized conveniently with bibliography in his "Covenant, Davidic," IDBSup, 188–92.

25. Weinfeld lifts up the place of the Abrahamic covenant promises (e.g. Genesis 12) in connection with the land aspect of the royal grants. The case for the interplay of the Abrahamic and Davidic traditions is well stated in R. E. Clements, *Abraham and David* (London: SCM Press, 1967), 47–60.

26. To the exclusion of loyalty in connection with the Mosaic covenant. Weinfeld, "Covenant, Davidic," IDBSup, 189.

27. Verse 52 is a general conclusion for Book III of the Psalter, not part of the original Psalm 89.

28. Artur Weiser, *The Psalms*, OTL (Philadelphia: Westminster Press, 1962), 590–91.

29. Whether this phrase is so closely tied to the Davidic covenant as Weinfeld suggests is open to question. His key examples are 1 Kings 8:23 and Deut. 7:12 (which he views as a reference to the Abrahamic covenant). But each of these verses can plausibly be related to the Sinai covenant (cf. Deut. 7:9) or to covenant tradition in an undifferentiated way. See p. 63, and n. 38 below. Other uses of this special expression occur in late and general contexts where Davidic rule is not particularly in view, namely, Neh. 9:32; Neh. 1:5; Dan. 9:4. These last two texts follow closely on Deut. 7:9 which is reminiscent of the Decalogue usage. Loyalty here is for the faithful; perpetuity is not at issue.

30. See Clements, *Abraham and David*, 47–60.

31. See chap. 2, "Stories of Human Loyalty," 30–32.

32. Kellenberger, *ḥäsäd*, 132–34.

33. Weiser, *Psalms*, 62.

34. Debate over the dating and provenance of the Deuteronomic history continues. While the outcome is not critical to our discussion here, I believe that F. M. Cross's "two-edition" approach is basically sound. See his *Canaanite Myth and Hebrew Epic* (Cambridge, Mass.: Harvard University Press, 1973), 274–89. This analysis has recently been supported and refined by, among others, Richard D. Nelson (*The Double Redaction of the Deuteronomistic History*, JSOTSup 18 [Sheffield: JSOT Press, 1981]) and Richard Elliott Friedman ("From Egypt to Egypt: Dtr[1] and Dtr[2]," in *Traditions in Transformation*, Halpern and Levenson). According to this analysis, the key material of 2 Samuel 7 comes from the historian writing during the reign of King Josiah, although the chapter may rely on extant liturgical tradition such as that preserved in Psalm 89.

35. The phrases about human reprisal are not intended to distinguish "ordinary" events from "miraculous" or "supernatural" happenings as we usually think of such distinctions today. The issue is rather penultimate versus ultimate judgment.

36. Especially in the Elijah-Elisha cycle (1 Kings 19; 21; 2 Kings 8; 9), but also Ahijah (1 Kings 11), Jehu ben Hanani (1 Kings 16:1–4), Micaiah (1 Kings 22). Cf. Hos. 8:4, and the study of W. F. Albright, *Samuel and the Beginnings of the Prophetic Movement* (Cincinnati: Hebrew Union College, 1961).

37. Nelson, *Double Redaction,* 100–105.

38. 1 Kings 8:23; 11:11; 2 Kings 11:17; 17:15, 35, 38; 23:3. Only the first two texts require clarifying interpretation. 1 Kings 8:23 is introductory to one section of Solomon's great prayer. Although v. 24 refers to the promise to David, the introduction is more general, implies loyalty only to the faithful, and uses "servants" in a plural which can readily refer to Yahweh worshipers generally rather than to the kings alone. In 1 Kings 11:11 it is true that Solomon alone is said not to have kept covenant and statutes; but precisely this statement indicates reference to the Mosaic tradition. The focus on going after other gods (v. 10) underlines this perspective.

39. These have been explored elsewhere in the Overtures to Biblical Theology series, by Ralph W. Klein, *Israel in Exile* (Philadelphia: Fortress Press, 1979).

40. Of course not everything in Second Isaiah is completely new. There are strong lines of thematic continuity with Isaiah of Jerusalem (chaps. 1—33) and also with the hymnic tradition of the Psalter. On the use of selected parts of the two covenant streams, see Bernhard W. Anderson, "Exodus and Covenant in Second Isaiah and Prophetic Tradition," in *Magnalia Dei, The Mighty Acts of God,* eds. F. M. Cross, W. Lemke, and P. Miller (Garden City, N.Y.: Doubleday & Co., 1975), 339–60; also Anderson's earlier essay, "Exodus Typology in Second Isaiah," in *Israel's Prophetic Heritage: Essays in Honor of James Muilenburg,* eds. B. W. Anderson and W. Harrelson (New York: Harper & Brothers, 1962), 177–95.

41. Some have seen in the servant poems (Isa. 42:1–4; 49:1–6; 50:4–11; 52:13—53:12) a messianic figure which could be related to the Davidic tradition. But the servant allusions outside of the poems are collective, referring to the whole community. For a convenient summary of the many options for understanding the servant of the poems, see John L. McKenzie, *Second Isaiah,* AB 20 (Garden City, N.Y.: Doubleday & Co., 1968), xliii–lv.

42. A classic exposition of this theme may be found in Otto Eissfeldt, "The Promises of Grace to David in Isaiah 55:1–5," in *Israel's Prophetic Heritage,* ed. Anderson and Harrelson (New York: Harper & Brothers, 1962), 196–207. For the vocation of David as heir to the promise to Abraham in the Yahwist epic tradition, see Clements, *Abraham and David,* 54–60.

43. See above, this chapter, 55–56.

44. The insidious working of the ancient imagery in our Western view of human relationships, leading to generalizations about dependency and unfaithfulness of women, is all too apparent. Having said this, in the next paragraphs I aim to convey the positive power of the image as it stands in the biblical text. Whether the image remains viable today is open to serious question. See chap. 5, "Loyalty: The Calling of the People of God," 112 n. 19.

45. See chap. 5, "Loyalty: The Calling of the People of God," 112–16.

46. On loyalty in Hos. 2:19b, see chap. 5, "Loyalty: The Calling of the People of God," 122–23.

47. Cf. Ezek. 34:25; 37:26; and especially Hos. 2:18, where in the marriage imagery context a new covenant is described as involving all creation and offering an end to war.

48. Only Isa. 16:5, a text replete with problems, associates loyalty with the (re?)establishment of the Davidic line.

49. It may be noted in passing that contemporary marriage counseling recognizes the need to deal with the lack of "closure" which may persist for years after a divorce.

50. In contrast to the Yahwist's adumbrations of the Davidic covenant and the various prophetic efforts to reassess the two covenant traditions.

51. If F. M. Cross (Canaanite Myth, 293–325) is correct that P incorporated JE as he wrote his narrative, then the case to be made here concerning loyalty in Numbers 13—14 relates directly to P's reuse of older tradition. If, on the other hand, as N. Lohfink has argued ("Die Priesterschrift und die Geschichte," Congress Volume: Göttingen, 1977, VTSup 29 [Leiden: E. J. Brill, 1978], 189–225), P was originally a separate narrative document, it would still seem that the combining redactor worked mainly from a P perspective. The perspective on loyalty would then be Priestly, but one step removed.

52. "Die Ursünden in der priesterlichen Geschichtserzählung," in Die Zeit Jesu, eds. G. Bornkamm and K. Rahner (Freiburg: Herder, 1970), 38–57. The first sin is the golden calf, the third is the disobedience of Moses and Aaron in the matter of water from the rock (Numbers 20).

53. For discussion of this problem and fuller treatment of the passage as a whole, see my "The Problem of Divine Forgiveness in Numbers 14," CBQ 37 (1975): 317–30.

54. Klein, Israel in Exile, 138.

CHAPTER 4

# Help in Need:
# God's Loyalty to Members of
# the Covenant Community

The expression "members of the covenant community" used in the
subtitle of this chapter is deliberately chosen for its ambiguity. The
phrase can refer in English to various individual Israelites one by
one, or it can refer to the totality of the community in a collective
sense. While the chapter concentrates particularly on texts referring to individuals, a neat or formal distinction between the individual and the community as a whole is inevitably artificial, especially for ancient Israel.[1] In the few biblical narratives that deal
specifically with God's loyalty to one individual, that loyalty regularly has important consequences for the larger community. So
also in the psalms, an individual petitioning for relief from distress
may recall God's past loyalty to the community in general, not
simply events from the petitioner's personal life. Likewise, God's
way of relating to the community as a whole is understood to have
very concrete implications for the lives of individuals within it,
whether they are confronting famine, warfare, or social injustice.
The individual's experience of loyalty as help in need is bound up
with the experience of the larger community. Whether deliverance,
protection, or forgiveness, biblical expressions of the content of
loyalty find their meaning for individuals within the context of the
covenant community.

In the richness of the Old Testament heritage, most of the texts
that describe loyalty as it was concretely experienced do not have
to be boxed into either one of the principal covenant categories
discussed in the preceding chapter. The prayers and narratives are

able to carry the double nuance of surprising faithfulness (God's loyalty is even greater than the recipient deserves or has any right to expect) and of promised faithfulness (God's loyalty can be counted upon no matter what). The refusal of the finally collected traditions of Israel to say either "surprise" or "promise" alone, the insistence that both themes are true, the willingness to emphasize whichever aspect is called for by the situation of the hearers—all of this can be seen in the biblical witness.

The preponderance of biblical testimony to God's loyalty to members of the Israelite community is found in the Psalter, with over seventy examples[2] scattered through more than forty-five of the psalms. There is some concentration of the references to loyalty in the psalms of lament[3] which are characterized by petition for assistance in the face of various kinds of distress, but the picture of divine loyalty manifest as help in need can be derived fom other psalm types as well. This chapter describes the salient features of such help in need experienced by those who belonged to Yahweh.

DELIVERANCE FROM ENEMIES

Perhaps the most common petition associated with desire for divine loyalty is the request for deliverance from enemies. As explicit as any is the concluding cry of Psalm 143:

> And in thy loyalty cut off my enemies,
>     and destroy all my adversaries,
>   for I am thy servant.
>                               (Ps. 143:12)

Psalm 17 states the petition more generally, but with equal force:

> Wondrously show thy loyalty,
>     O savior of those who seek refuge
>     from their adversaries at thy right hand.
>                               (Ps. 17:7)

Other prayers for deliverance from enemies refer to God's loyalty, not in the petition section itself, but in a section of the psalm that affirms the petitioner's trust that the response of God will be made manifest:

He will send from heaven and save me,
　he will put to shame those who trample upon me.
God will send forth his loyalty and his faithfulness!
                                  (Ps. 57:3)

In some instances the expression of trust in divine loyalty closely anticipates the time when deliverance will have been received and rejoicing in the rescue will commence:

But I have trusted in thy loyalty;
　my heart shall rejoice in thy salvation.
                                  (Ps. 13:5)

Still other prayers refer to loyalty in the setting of the "vow of praise," the promise that the petitioner will give thanksgiving to God for the rescue which will be received:

I will rejoice and be glad for thy loyalty,
　because thou hast seen my affliction,
　thou hast taken heed of my adversities,
and hast not delivered me into the hand of the enemy;
　thou hast set my feet in a broad place.
                                  (Ps. 31:7–8)

But I through the abundance of thy loyalty
　will enter thy house,
I will worship toward thy holy temple
　in the fear of thee.
                                  (Ps. 5:7)

Psalm 138 illustrates the prayer of thanksgiving offered after the deliverance:

I bow down toward thy holy temple
　and give thanks to thy name for thy sure loyalty.
                                  (Ps. 138:2a)

These appeals to God for loyalty in the form of deliverance expand upon the theme of rescue from serious distress which proved typical of the narratives about human loyalty discussed in chapter 2, "Stories of Human Loyalty." Unable to secure safety in the ordinary course of events, the psalmist turns to One more powerful than either petitioner or enemy. Help is sought in time of dire need. Although the psalms are general enough in their imagery to encompass a wide variety of trouble, in nearly every case the prayer suggests that life itself or at least normal life is at stake in the outcome: "deliver my life" (Ps. 17:13); "our soul is bowed down to the dust" (Ps. 44:25); "those who trample upon me" (Ps. 57:3); "preserve my life" (Ps. 143:11). The enemies are a serious threat; the psalmist's petition is urgent, not casual or general.

The appeal to divine loyalty in a life-threatening individual situation appears also in the Jacob narrative of Genesis 32. As Jacob returns from Aram and reaches the Jabbok River, he hears that Esau is coming to meet him with four hundred men. He is "greatly afraid" and prays to God, beginning with a reminder that his returning is at God's own suggestion. He continues:

> I am not worthy of the least of all the sure loyalty which thou hast shown to thy servant. . . . Deliver me, I pray thee, . . . from the hand of Esau, for I fear him, lest he come and slay us all, the mothers with the children. (Gen. 32:10–11)

The prayer incorporates an indirect protestation of righteousness (in its reference to Jacob's obedience in returning from Aram), a recollection of God's previous benefits, and a reminder to God of yet unfulfilled divine promises. Jacob attributes his prospering to God's loyalty and prays that he can count on Yahweh to follow through for him on this dangerous occasion. Loyalty manifest in family and flocks is meaningless if it is suddenly to be cut off. Rescue from Esau will open the way to continued fulfillment of the divine promise of many descendants. While divine loyalty under-girds all that makes life meaningful, it comes to special expression when Jacob's well-being is threatened. God's loyalty manifest to Jacob in Esau's favorable welcome becomes, in the long run, loyalty for all Israel as well; for it is the patronymic ancestor Israel together with his children, the tribal heads, whom God delivers. Without divine loyalty at this juncture, there would have been no people of Israel.

Both the Genesis 32 reference to "sure" loyalty and the various psalm texts suggest that loyalty refers both to an *attitude,* which serves as the basis for faithful action in the relationship between God and the petitioners, and also to the rescuing *action* itself. The two themes are caught up together in expressions such as, "Show forth thy loyalty," or, "God will send forth his loyalty and his faithfulness." Prepositional constructions such as "for the sake of thy loyalty" or "in thy loyalty" draw attention more to God's attitude as basis for the prayed-for deliverance. But the contexts repeatedly testify that loyalty is never something purely abstract or intangible. If loyalty does not issue in appropriate action, then it has faded away or ceased to exist. Loyalty is tested and measured in situations of particular need and so is not usually mentioned in connection with the general good life under God's blessing which the faithful experience in day-to-day living. Loyalty may take shape in general sustenance, but it is most often noted in times of distress.

Particularly in the psalms, God's loyalty to the faithful is often associated with dire consequences for the "enemies" who have brought on all the trouble. Most Christian liturgical use of the Psalter avoids these texts about enemies; but to take divine loyalty seriously requires that one come to grips with these petitions. What theological sense can be made of such passages? How might they be related to the New Testament commandment, "Love your enemies"?

The "enemies" may be individual or national, private or public, economic or political or religious opponents. Most often the language about enemies is general enough to allow people in quite varied situations to pray the same psalm. As many modern commentators have pointed out, these enemies ought not to be "spiritualized" as internal forces or private moral struggles. The psalmists are talking about real, flesh-and-blood troublemakers who are ruining their individual or corporate lives in very concrete ways.[4] And there is no denying that these psalms are full of suggestions to God for all kinds of disasters which could befall the enemies: confront them, overthrow them, put them to shame, cut them off, cast them out, destroy them, let them fall into their own pit, let them fall by their own counsel. Vengeance, not love, seems to be the rule.

In the context of this study, the problem is to understand the loyalty of God which seems to favor one group at the expense of another, to rescue one by destroying another. Theologically speaking, can we affirm or appropriate this kind of loyalty? Is there a context that can help us either to modify or to appreciate such a perception of divine loyalty?

It is important in the first place to recognize that the psalmist regularly understands the enemy to be actively opposed to God's will. The psalmist as a person of faith is attempting to live righteously, and that effort is being thwarted by the enemy. Thus, while the psalmist speaks of "my" enemy, the enemy is properly understood to be the enemy of God as well. "They have rebelled against *thee*," says the petitioner (Ps. 5:10, italics added). In calling God's attention to the enemies' rebellion, the speaker pleads for the exercise of divine justice in loyal vindication of the faithful. To undo the wicked opponent would be to reestablish divine order:

> From thee let my vindication come!
>   Let thy eyes see the right!
>                    (Ps. 17:2)

Furthermore, the form of the prayer leaves the action up to God. The petitioner does not ask, "Show me how to undo the enemy." Divine action is called for partly because the persecuted petitioner has exhausted all human resources and can see no way out. While it would be wrong to suppose that no human agency would ever be involved in divine response to the prayer, the consistent picture of divine judgment in the downfall of the enemies reinforces the understanding of these enemies as the enemies of God. "The Lord preserves the faithful, but abundantly requites [the one] who acts haughtily" (Ps. 31:23).

It is true that there are no petitions for forgiveness of the enemies, and no petitions focus on their transformation rather than on their confounding. Reflecting on God's care for all people invites one to supplement the psalmist's petitions with petitions of these types. But in my view the petitions of the psalms are not inappropriate for contemporary use. They express honestly our innermost attitudes about our enemies (as if God did not know them already!). They express the focus on our own need which comes to the fore when we are so hard pressed that we can scarcely pray for ourselves, much less for anyone else. And most especially, they take seriously the depth of evil and perversity which opposes God's way and which thwarts us personally and corporately as we try to live faithfully with our sisters and brothers. Those who pray, "Thy kingdom come, thy will be done, . . . deliver us from evil," join with the psalmist's "Make haste to answer me. . . . Teach me to do thy will . . . , and in thy loyalty cut off my enemies" (Ps. 143:7, 10, 12). God's sure loyalty to the faithful provides the basis for hope that righteousness will be established in the community and indeed upon the earth.

PROTECTION

Very closely related to specific petitions for deliverance are prayers for protection as help in need appropriate to divine loyalty. Indeed, several of the psalms cited above speak of protection in other strophes, while some of those to be mentioned here include petitions for deliverance in other sections. The distinction in category is made here primarily to emphasize that loyalty may be shown and experienced concretely in a durative way, not only in episodic acts of rescue or deliverance.

Among the clearer examples of this protection theme is the concluding vow of praise in the lament of Psalm 59:

> But I will sing of thy might;
> I will sing aloud of thy loyalty in the morning.
> For thou hast been to me a fortress
> and a refuge in the day of my distress.
>                                          (Ps. 59:16)

The prayer overall is one for deliverance, but the theme of loyalty is associated especially with God's ongoing protection when the enemies return repeatedly to seek their prey (Ps. 59:6–10).

Psalm 32 praises God for recovery from illness which is associated with forgiveness of sin. The psalmist concludes with a summary statement of the basis for rejoicing among the upright in heart:

> Many are the pangs of the wicked;
> but loyalty surrounds [the one] who trusts in the Lord.
>                                          (Ps. 32:10)

Earlier in the psalm, God is spoken of as hiding place and as preserver from trouble (Ps. 32:7), two images of divine protection. Here in the summary this same theme is evoked again by the unusual verb "surrounds,"[5] with loyalty as the verb subject.

The theme of ongoing protection appears also in the petition of Ps. 40:11:

> Let thy loyalty and faithfulness
> ever preserve me!

Both the adverb "ever" and the verb "preserve," with its connotation of guarding from danger, highlight the durative character of the experience of God's loyalty. In the present form of Psalm 40, this verse provides the transition from a prayer of thanksgiving for deliverance to a new prayer of petition for deliverance. While the motif of protection could be appropriate to either portion of the psalm, it is especially striking in this transitional position. It suggests how the many single acts of rescue in which God's loyalty is experienced add up to (or better, are evidence of) ongoing protection and preservation as a deeper and broader expression of that loyalty. This movement from the episodic to the durative underscores the conjoining of the attitudinal dimension with the dimension of concrete action in the biblical conception of loyalty.

Several narratives that relate God's loyalty to individuals lift up this dual focus on attitude and action and also illustrate protection in its broadest sense, in which Yahweh does what is needful to make the situation "come round right." These stories involve Joseph, Abraham, and the family of Ruth.

Through the false testimony of Potiphar's wife, the young man Joseph is cast into prison. It seems to be just one more incident in the series of disasters that have befallen him.

> But the Lord was with Joseph and showed him loyalty, and gave him favor in the sight of the keeper of the prison. (Gen. 39:21)

So Joseph is put in charge of the prison. The theme of God's being with Joseph runs throughout this story, but it is when he is in the most serious trouble that divine assistance is described as loyalty. Here we see both God's attitude and how that attitude took on concrete form. This juncture is critical in the narrative, for

Joseph's assignment gives him contact with the man who eventually has him brought before the king of Egypt, who makes him vizier of the land. As vizier, Joseph eventually saves his own family; God's loyalty to one individual has consequences for the covenant community as a whole.

In the same way, the journey of Abraham's servant to find a wife from the home country for Isaac represents a critical juncture in the patriarchal tradition. Although it may seem a light matter to many modern folk, purity of bloodline was of the utmost consequence in the traditional culture of Israel. The theological setting of the patriarchal promise of multitudinous progeny further heightens the significance of the servant's mission; from Israel's point of view, the promise itself is at stake. Again loyalty is the work of God to bring to a good ending a situation full of uncertainty for the future (not only for Abraham and Isaac but also for the covenant people). The servant stops to pray as he arrives at a well in the homeland:

> O Lord, God of my master Abraham, grant me success today, I pray thee, and show loyalty to my master Abraham. . . . Let the maiden to whom I shall say . . . [detailed criteria follow]—let her be the one whom thou hast appointed for thy servant Isaac. By this I shall know that thou hast shown loyalty to my master. (Gen. 24:12–14)

Before the servant even finishes the prayer, Rebekah appears and fulfills all the criteria he has set forth. When he learns that she is indeed of Abraham's kin he prays again:

> Blessed be the Lord, the God of my master Abraham, who has not forsaken his sure loyalty toward my master. (Gen. 24:27)

The wording of both prayers makes clear that it is divine loyalty to the patriarch Abraham which is at stake—Abraham's need for a suitable daughter-in-law is the centerpiece; the servant's need to find the right young woman is only instrumental to the main issue. Yet it is through that very practical process that Abraham receives divine loyalty and the story comes round right. The specific happening that enables the identification of the designated young woman bears witness to the constancy of Yahweh's loyal attitude toward Abraham.

As in the preceding examples, God's loyalty to individuals in the story of Ruth has momentous consequences for the life of the covenant community. When Ruth comes home from her first day of gleaning and reports that she has been in the field belonging to Boaz, Naomi exclaims:

> Blessed be he by Yahweh, who has not abandoned his loyalty with the living or the dead! (Ruth 2:20, au. trans.)[6]

Here, as in each of the other narratives, God has initiated the sequence of events that lead to favorable resolution of a precarious situation. Divine loyalty as an attitude (something "not abandoned") is recognized afresh in Yahweh's response to the situation of need. The specific incident rekindles Naomi's almost extinguished confidence in the loyalty of Yahweh, loyalty which had endured even though her trust in it had failed in the bitterness of her loss of family.

Naomi's exclamation reflects Yahweh's role in what the narrator has told the reader already:

> And [Ruth] happened to come to the part of the field belonging to Boaz, who was of the family of Elimelech. (Ruth 2:3)

Ruth "happened to come," but it happened in the loyalty of God. Naomi's allusion to loyalty toward the dead (her husband and sons) very subtly foreshadows the conclusion of the narrative in which the town women rejoice over Ruth's baby with the words, "A son is born to Naomi." Through Ruth's marriage to Boaz, both the economic security of the two women and the perpetuation of Elimelech's line are provided for. And in the end all Israel benefits as well, for the child Obed was grandfather to King David.[7]

A final example of loyalty made known in general protection is found in Psalm 33, a hymn praising Yahweh, who created the universe and who, enthroned in heaven, looks down upon all the deeds of peoples and nations. The psalmist proclaims the value of trust in God and the uselessness of any plans or military might contrary to Yahweh's will. The psalm continues:

> Behold, the eye of the Lord is on those who fear him,
>   on those who hope in his loyalty,

HELP IN NEED    93

that he may deliver their soul from death,
   and keep them alive in famine.
                              (Ps. 33:18–19)

This assertion is beautifully paired with the concluding petition:

Let thy loyalty, O Lord, be upon us,
   even as we hope in thee.
                              (Ps. 33:22)

The eye of the Lord is upon those who hope in divine loyalty; divine loyalty is asked upon those who hope in the Lord. The upright are called to count upon divine faithfulness, to trust in the trustworthiness of their God. Such hope and trust is based in the confidence that Yahweh is Help and Shield (v. 20) who indeed shows loyal care to those who wait eagerly for the divine work done in faithfulness (v. 4). In all the vicissitudes of international diplomacy and warfare (vv. 10–17), Yahweh the creator of all, the loyal One (vv. 6–9) is mindful of the faithful and offers them divine protection.

FORGIVENESS

We have seen in chapter 3, "Freedom and Commitment," that loyalty manifest as forgiveness in the covenant traditions of Israel focused on the preservation of the entire community as the people of Yahweh. In the Mosaic covenant tradition the continuing of Yahweh's relationship to Israel despite their sin was ever surprising, rooted in the abounding loyalty of the God who nevertheless regarded sin with radical seriousness. In the Davidic covenant tradition, Yahweh's promised relationship with the king was predicated upon the limitation of punishment to "human rods and stripes," so that king and people would ever stand before God.

Just as deliverance and protection are sought for individual members of the community, as well as for the people as a whole, so also forgiveness is asked and received by members of the community as manifestation of divine loyalty. Often the hope for restoration of right relationship to God is associated with a plea for deliverance from some distress that has been interpreted as a sign of divine displeasure.

Psalm 6, the first of the seven so-called "penitential" psalms,[8] presents a straightforward request for the sparing of life:

> Turn, O Lord, save my life;
>   deliver me for the sake of thy loyalty.
> For in death there is no remembrance of thee;
>   in Sheol who can give thee praise?
>                     (Ps. 6:4–5)

The context surrounding these verses alludes both to illness ("Heal me, for my bones are troubled," v. 2) and to external foes ("All my enemies shall be ashamed and sorely troubled," v. 10), but the overarching theme is traditionally taken from the opening line:

> O Lord, rebuke me not in thy anger.
>                     (Ps. 6:1)

The direct association of the appeal to God's loyalty in v. 4 is with deliverance, but the setting suggests that deliverance will signify/result from the turning aside of God's wrath from the suppliant.

Similarly, in the middle of Psalm 143 the petitioner exhorts:

> Hide not thy face from me,
>   lest I be like those who go down to the Pit.
> Let me hear in the morning of thy loyalty,
>   for in thee I put my trust.
>                     (Ps. 143:7b–8a)

In this psalm also enemy oppression (vv. 3, 9, 12) and recognition of the suppliant's unrighteousness (v. 2) are brought together. The granting of respite from trouble may be interpreted as God's forgiving response to the renewed trust of the prayerful servant.

As Weiser has pointed out, Psalms 6 and 143 are penitential only by indirection, with the theme suggested in the opening lines of each.[9] Neither psalm actually contains an explicit confession of sin; the connection between loyalty and forgiveness is only implicit, since the word "loyalty" itself is connected in each case with the plea for deliverance from distress.

A different pattern appears in Psalms 86 and 103. Although the petitioner is not pictured as a penitent in these psalms, the prayer nevertheless asks for help on the basis of God's forgiving nature, which is explicitly based in God's loyalty. In a petition for deliverance from enemies, the suppliant offers this reason:

> For thou, O Lord, art good and forgiving,
> abounding in loyalty to all who call on thee.
>
> (Ps. 86:5)

The allusion to the liturgical tradition of the name of God of Exodus 33 is clear; it is cited more fully toward the end of the psalm:

> But thou, O Lord, art a God merciful and gracious,
> slow to anger and abounding in sure loyalty.
>
> (Ps. 86:15)

The connection between loyalty and forgiveness is direct, but the need of the petitioner for forgiveness is known only on the basis of these general allusions within the psalm.

Psalm 103, a thanksgiving to God, also refers to Yahweh's loyal forgiveness in a general way. The prayer begins with the familiar lines:

> Bless the Lord, O my soul;
> and all that is within me,
> bless his holy name!
> Bless the Lord, O my soul,
> and forget not all his benefits,
> who forgives all your iniquity,
> who heals all your diseases,
> who redeems your life from the Pit,
> who crowns you with loyalty and mercy,
>
> (Ps. 103:1–4)

The psalm continues with allusion to the divine revelation to Moses and Israel at Sinai and a variation on the liturgical tradition of Exodus 33 which makes God's forgiving nature very explicit:

> The Lord is merciful and gracious,
> slow to anger and abounding in loyalty.
> He will not always chide,
> nor will he keep his anger for ever.
> He does not deal with us according to our sins,
> nor requite us according to our iniquities.

> For as the heavens are high above the earth,
> so great is his loyalty toward those who fear him;
> as far as the east is from the west,
> so far does he remove our transgressions from us.
>
> (Ps. 103:8–12)

The forgiveness implicitly extended in God's healing of the individual praying the psalm is thus set into the larger context of divine loyalty to the entire community and all its members. The individual's experience is both illustration and confirmation of the character of God's loyal forgiving of all the people.

Yet a third pattern appears in Psalms 25 and 51, where God's loyalty is directly associated with the penitent's explicit plea for forgiveness. The familiar opening lines of Psalm 51 make the point clearly:

> Have mercy on me, O God,
> according to thy loyalty;
> according to thy abundant mercy
> blot out my transgressions.
>
> (Ps. 51:1)

Loyalty is the basis for mercy, which in turn is the ground for forgiveness. The psalm continues with explicit confession, recognition of the justice of God, and request for cleansing and restoration. Here, as in Psalms 86 and 103, divine loyalty is regarded as the basis for the restoring of right relationship with God, for binding up that which has been broken by human failure. But here in Psalm 51 this understanding is applied very explicitly to the individual petitioner.

Psalm 25 is like Psalm 51 in its inclusion of specific appeals for forgiveness (25:7, 11, 18) and also in its explicit appeal to divine loyalty as the ground for forgiveness:

> Be mindful of thy mercy, O Lord, and of thy loyalty,
> for they have been from of old.
> Remember not the sins of my youth, or my transgressions;
> according to thy loyalty remember me,
> for thy goodness' sake, O Lord!
>
> (Ps. 25:6–7)

The specific plea for forgiveness is, in this case, accompanied by an appeal for deliverance from enemies:[10]

Consider how many are my foes,
 and with what violent hatred they hate me.
Oh guard my life, and deliver me;
 let me not be put to shame, for I take refuge in thee.
                                          (Ps. 25:19–20)

The concluding phrase, "for I take refuge in thee," offers a key to understanding an apparent tension within Psalm 25, a tension which is also much in evidence in Psalm 103. In both prayers, divine loyalty is recognized as the basis for any hope of forgiveness (25:6–7; 103:8–10). Yet in each case the psalmist also insists that God's loyalty is restricted to the faithful who keep Yahweh's covenant:

But the loyalty of the Lord is from everlasting to everlasting
 upon those who fear him,
 and his righteousness to children's children,
to those who keep his covenant
 and remember to do his commandments.
                                          (Ps. 103:17–18)

All the paths of the Lord are sure loyalty,
 for those who keep his covenant and his testimonies.
                                          (Ps. 25:10)

These restrictive statements are reminiscent of the "conditional loyalty" of the Mosaic covenant theology, while the "forgiving loyalty" of the Mosaic tradition characterizes the other verses of these psalms. The resolution of this tension lies in the repeated statements of the petitioner's trust in Yahweh which are typical of the psalms of lament generally. So in Psalm 25 the suppliant states, "In thee I trust" (v. 2), "For thee I wait" (vv. 5, 21), "My eyes are ever toward the Lord" (v. 15), "I take refuge in thee" (v. 20). The very fact that the petitioner is turning to God in prayer and asking for forgiveness identifies the person as one who desires to be instructed by God (v. 12) so as to keep the covenant. The affirmation of trust becomes the petitioner's basis for asking divine forgiveness. By such statements of trust the penitents place themselves in the same status before God as the innocent petitioners who make such declarations of trust in other psalms of lament.[11]

This common declaration of trust helps also to explain why the borderline between "penitential" and other petitionary psalms is so fuzzy. God's loyalty is indeed offered in support of the faithful, but that loyalty so abounds that those who have fallen away can yet dare to hope that they will not be cast away from God's presence (Ps. 51:11) but may still be counted again as among the covenant keepers, who find their communal identity in God's presence with them. For the individual member of the community, as for the people as a whole, Yahweh's loyalty experienced in forgiveness undergirds every other manifestation of that loyalty. Psalm 32 states the point succinctly:

Blessed is [the one] whose transgression is forgiven,
    whose sin is covered.

. . . . . . . . . .

When I declared not my sin, my body wasted away
    through my groaning all day long.

. . . . . . . . . . . . . . .

I said, "I will confess my transgressions to the Lord";
    then thou didst forgive the guilt of my sin.

. . . . . . . . . . . . . . . . . .

Many are the pangs of the wicked;
    but loyalty surrounds [the one] who trusts in the Lord.
Be glad in the Lord, and rejoice, O righteous,
    and shout for joy, all you upright in heart!
                  (Ps. 32:1, 3, 5b, 10–11)

## NOTES

1. See the classic essay of H. Wheeler Robinson, *Corporate Personality in Ancient Israel* (Philadelphia: Fortress Press, 1964).

2. Not counting the repetitions of the refrain "his loyalty endures for ever."

3. For a succinct discussion of the types of psalms, see Bernhard W. Anderson, *Out of the Depths: The Psalms Speak for Us Today,* Revised and Expanded Edition (Philadelphia: Westminster Press, 1983). The concentration of loyalty references in the psalms of lament has been discussed by Thorir K. Thordarson, "The Form-Historical Problem of Ex. 34:6–7" (unpublished Ph.D. dissertation, University of Chicago Divinity School, 1959), 150ff. One should be cautious about the significance of this "concentration," however. Twenty-six (or about half) of the psalms that refer to loyalty are of the lament type, using Anderson's typology; but more than one-third of the psalms (about sixty) fall into this lament category. This

means both that loyalty is not specifically mentioned in the majority of laments and also that the word is not infrequent among other psalm types. The psalms praise God's loyalty as well as appealing to it; they give thanks for it and declare trust in it.

4. Erhard S. Gerstenberger has emphasized the this-worldly individual and corporate aspects of conflict and oppression in his "Enemies and Evildoers in the Psalms: A Challenge to Christian Preaching," *Horizons in Biblical Theology* 4–5 (1982–83): 61–77.

5. The *po'el* form of *sbb* used here is relatively infrequent. Closest thematically to the usage here is Deut. 32:10, which speaks of God's encircling care of Israel in the wilderness.

6. This translation makes clearer than the RSV that Yahweh's loyalty (more than Boaz's) is in focus here. The Greek and also parallel Hebrew constructions support this interpretation, as does the position of Naomi's exclamation within the plot sequence. Boaz has not yet done anything readily viewed as loyalty by the criteria developed in the discussion of human loyalty in chap. 2, "Stories of Human Loyalty." In any case, Naomi responds only to the name itself, for Ruth has not yet told her anything of what Boaz has said.

7. Ruth's loyalty to Naomi and the entire family of Elimelech in marrying Boaz was discussed in chap. 2, "Stories of Human Loyalty." The interplay between Yahweh's loyalty and Ruth's in this beautiful narrative anticipates the broader biblical meaning of living loyally which will be developed in chap. 5, "Loyalty: The Calling of the People of God."

8. Psalms 6; 32; 38; 51; 102; 130; 143. God's loyalty is mentioned explicitly in four of these: Psalms 6; 32; 51; and 143. There are other psalms that include reference to God's forgiveness (such as Psalms 25; 86; 103) but are not included in the traditional penitential group. A careful reading of the psalms makes clear how difficult it is in many cases to categorize them according to the innocent or penitential status of the suppliant.

9. Artur Weiser, *The Psalms*, OTL (Philadelphia: Westminster Press, 1962), 130, 818.

10. Of the six psalms considered in this section, only Psalm 51 lacks an explicit reference to deliverance from some sort of "external" distress such as illness or enemies. Our modern tendency is often to restrict the concept of divine forgiveness to private and interior consequences, more along the lines of Psalm 51. Probably we restrict forgiveness in this way partly because we find the idea of suffering as God's judgment so difficult to work with theologically. Studies such as Daniel Simundson's *Faith Under Fire: Biblical Interpretations of Suffering* (Minneapolis: Augsburg Publishing House, 1980) and W. Sibley Towner's *How God Deals with Evil* (Philadelphia: Westminster Press, 1976) are among several recent works addressing

this issue. Indeed, we should be careful not to construe every human misfortune as evidence of divine judgment. Israel itself recognized many disastrous circumstances as the havoc wreaked by human sin upon innocent victims. Each situation required individual evaluation; the Book of Job portrays the danger of interpreting every disaster in a single way.

11. This use of the declaration of trust is related theologically to the function of the declarations of righteousness studied by Gerhard von Rad in " 'Righteousness' and 'Life' in the Cultic Language of the Psalms," in *The Problem of the Hexateuch and Other Essays* (New York: McGraw-Hill Book Co., 1966), 243–66. Von Rad showed that the seemingly exaggerated claims of righteousness do not refer to moral perfection at all, but rather have to do with faithfulness in relationship to God. Such claims, which include also declarations of perfect trust, are liturgical language "prescribed by the cultus as a means of obtaining the favor God has offered to Israel" (p. 250).

# CHAPTER 5

# Loyalty:
# The Calling of
# the People of God

Many biblical narratives speak of acts of individual loyalty shown by one person to another. As we have seen in chapter 2, "Stories of Human Loyalty," loyalty in such narratives functions in the realm of ordinary human relationships in the personal and political spheres; in most of these passages the word does not have any overt religious connotation. By contrast, there are relatively few, scarcely a dozen, texts that consider human loyalty from a specifically religious point of view. From these few but very important texts we may learn something of the way in which Israel interpreted human loyalty as a component of life lived faithfully before God.

## TO LOVE LOYALTY

The most famous of the calls for loyalty as a quality befitting Yahweh worshipers is found in Micah:

> He has showed you, O man, what is good;
>   and what does the Lord require of you
> but to do justice, and to love loyalty,
>   and to walk humbly with your God?
>                (Mic. 6:8)

A study of the context lends fresh power and meaning to these familiar lines. The words are given as answer to the question of v. 6:

> With what shall I come before the Lord?
>                (Mic. 6:6)

As James L. Mays suggests, the setting underlying the form of
vv. 6–8 is that of the layperson (presumably male, see this chapter,
103 n. 7) approaching a cultic official for information about a
proper course of religious action.[1] The usual respondent would be
a priest, as the subject matter of proper sacrificial offering indicates. The inquirer wants to atone for sin by sufficient sacrifice:
and the prophet underlines his point by portraying the inquirer
going to absurd lengths in suggesting impossible quantities of
sacrifice ("thousands of rams . . . , rivers of oil") and even a first-
born child (v. 7). In stark contrast comes the answer: "He has
showed you . . ."—you should already know what is required. As
Mays sums up the reply, "It's you, not something, God wants."[2]
Conduct, life style, is the proper focus for the penitent. The
question about sacrifice is misdirected, for what is required is
radical repentance. What would such a life style look like?

In the preceding chapters we have seen that loyalty, whether
divine or human, involves aid for the circumstantially weaker and
needy party in a relationship. Here the sphere of relationship for
the inquirer should be taken as all those individuals with whom
daily life brings direct contact, and, even beyond that, the covenant community as a whole. Loyalty involves active concern for
the well-being of all the people of God,[3] but particularly for the
weak and underprivileged among them—the poor or any whose
status offers no ready advocate in the society. Being concerned for
God's requirement "to do justice" means especially to see to the
impartiality of juridical decisions (Deut. 1:17). Doing justice provides one important channel for showing loyalty even beyond one's
own circle of acquaintance. But precisely to achieve such operation
of justice, special concern needs to be shown for the least members
of the community. The law provided, for instance, for care of the
landless (the sojourner, orphan, or widow) through gleaning
(Deut. 24:19–21), or for adequate clothing for the poor through
returning for the night hours a cloak taken in collateral (Exod.
22:26–27). If such laws were broken, the victims would scarcely be
in a position to protest. It is an attitude of loyalty, with its special
concern for such disadvantaged people, that would support the
observance of such traditions and so undergird the possibility of

justice for *all* (including the powerless) and hence a *shalom* (whole, peace-filled) community.[4]

But the concept of loyalty involves more than supporting the weak, whether through acts of rescue or through preventive protection. Loyalty implies also the free taking on of that obligation to the other, even though the responsibility could easily be shirked. The prophet's choice of verb, "to *love* loyalty," underlines this aspect of the radically repentant life which God seeks. Support for the weak will not be offered grudgingly or out of fear of divine reprisal, as if the life style itself were to be equated with a material offering for sin. It will be willingly done because of a sense of commitment (obligation) to those others in community. It will grow out of an attitude toward community which takes the powerless as seriously as it takes those to whom it might "pay" to be nice.[5] This is not to say that loyalty involves completely spontaneous action. The action that loyalty calls for is generally costly; so loyalty requires constant reflection and renewed commitment. In his exhortation to "love loyalty," the prophet catches up both the attitude that befits the true Yahweh worshiper and the kind of concrete consequences that can be expected to issue from that world view.

This dimension of commitment and reflection is reinforced by the summarizing expression, "to walk humbly with your God." The verb means to walk wisely or circumspectly, or with discernment. As Mays puts it:

> It is a way of life that is humble, not so much by self-effacement, as by considered attention to another. The humility lies in not going one's own way presumptuously, but in attending the will and way of God. Israel's God performs and seeks justice and mercy; the "humble" walk with him in that course.[6]

The position of vv. 6–8 immediately following upon a partial "covenant lawsuit" which opens Micah 6 lends an additional dimension to the text. At one level, vv. 6–8 present the questioner as though a single inquiring penitent were involved. Of course such a personification can represent any/every Israelite.[7] But in conjunction with v. 2 the inquirer is also to be viewed as all-Israel, as the whole covenant community viewed collectively. The "covenant lawsuit" imagery, rooted in the Sinai covenant tradition, portrays Yahweh as plaintiff and Israel as defendant in a juridical proceeding. Yahweh recalls all the gracious acts of caring that the vassal has received,[8] and asks rhetorically on what basis Israel has found reason to violate the covenant. Then vv. 6–8, in rough analogy to international treaty procedure, suggest that no amount of tribute is meaningful unless the vassal also maintains allegiance to the suzerain. The juridical motif thus is modified; and the cultic question functions here at a second level on the analogy of a warning notice in the sphere of international diplomacy.[9]

Loyalty, then, is something which the community as a whole must love and live out; it is more than the obligation of each individual one by one. Furthermore, the juridical/diplomatic metaphor of the covenant lawsuit suggests that loyalty might even be part of the allegiance which Israel owes to God. This last suggestion may sound quite ordinary, because English usage so readily speaks of loyalty of the vassal to the suzerain. But in the light of the biblical meaning of loyalty developed in the preceding chapters, this suggestion in fact sounds very peculiar, because we have seen that loyalty in the biblical sense is precisely *not* what the weaker does for the stronger. What is the significance of this peculiar nuance of Israel's loyalty *as allegiance to God* in the covenant context? The prophet Hosea offers additional clues.

Hosea's prophecy is the earliest material that incorporates any reference to Israel's covenantal loyalty. The term "loyalty" occurs six times in this relatively brief prophetic book, a concentration of usage which is elsewhere approached only in the Psalter. And all of these six texts concern Israel's loyalty as the covenant community. There are no texts in Hosea which speak of God's loyalty to Israel.[10] This skewed distribution is in itself striking, given Hosea's roots within the Mosaic covenant tradition and the role of divine loyalty in that tradition. In Hosea, then, something new is afoot, which is reflected also in Micah 6 and in Jeremiah (both chronologically later than Hosea).

## WHAT GOD DESIRES

Hosea 6:1–6 refers to loyalty in a context that has strong thematic affinities with the Micah text discussed above. The opening

three verses of Hosea 6 are the words of the people who propose to
seek God in a time of distress:

> Come, let us return to the Lord;
>> for he has torn, that he may heal us;
>> he has stricken, and he will bind us up.
> After two days he will revive us;
>> on the third day he will raise us up,
>> that we may live before him.
> Let us know, let us press on to know the Lord;
>> his going forth is sure as the dawn;
> he will come to us as the showers,
>> as the spring rains that water the earth.
>> (Hos. 6:1–3)

The phrases probably reflect a litany form with some lines to be
recited by the priestly leadership and others by the congregation.
These words of repentance have been variously characterized as
hypocritical words of the community, sincere words of the community, or a sarcastic composition by Hosea.[11] The most probable
interpretation, in my view, is that the priests and the people say
these words sincerely, but Hosea recognizes that despite this sin-
cerity the litany does not constitute a proper theological basis for
returning to Yahweh. The inadequacy is seen subtly, in the over-
reaching certainty that God will respond in a prescribed manner, in
the allusions to mythological motifs, and in the use of nature
imagery which is beautiful in itself but which in the specific situation of Baal apostasy suggests that Yahweh is still being subsumed
under the Canaanite fertility religion which Hosea opposes.

Verses 4–6 give Yahweh's reply to the people's penitential words.
The divine response relates only indirectly to what has gone before, but in its indirection it points all the more strongly to the real
issue at hand:

> What shall I do with you, O Ephraim?
>> What shall I do with you, O Judah?
> Your loyalty is like a morning cloud,
>> like the dew that goes early away.
> Therefore I have hewn them by the prophets,
>> I have slain them by the words of my mouth,
>> and my judgment goes forth as the light.

> For I desire loyalty and not sacrifice,
> the knowledge of God, rather than burnt offerings.
>                                          (Hos. 6:4–6)

The opening questions portray the frustration of the caring deity who sees a wayward people wanting to return yet somehow unable to recognize the right path. The image of loyalty as evaporating dew plays against the nature imagery of the preceding litany. The people had spoken of Yahweh as sure as the rains, not sensing that the rain itself depended upon God; now their behavior is contrasted as short-lived or transitory rather than sure. The comparison to dew also plays on the concept of loyalty itself. Loyalty by definition has to do with carrying through on commitment; the image portrays a people who make a good start but fall by the wayside. Since God's words come in response to a litany of repentance, the ephemeral loyalty spoken of refers to Israel's renewed turning to Yahweh, who laments that their repentance is not to be counted upon because they have not yet really understood what is at stake. The past history of God's dealings with the people in prophetic proclamation and judgment confirms the transitory character of their responses and the legitimacy of Yahweh's frustration. The climactic lines of v. 6 then, like Mic. 6:8, exhort the people to God's true desire—loyalty (which is not fickle) and knowledge of God.

Although the contrast to sacrifice and burnt offerings is explicit here as well as in Micah, the point is not the dismantling of the ancient sacrificial system. Rather, Hosea and Micah alike emphasize that God's favor cannot be bought with such material offerings. Although the litany of Hos. 6:1–3 does not specifically propose to offer sacrifice, the mythological framework and theme of guaranteed divine response suggest that ritual was more on the people's minds than life style. A century later Jeremiah would voice in Yahweh's name this same concern:

> Amend your ways and your doings, and I will let you dwell in this place. Do not trust in these deceptive words: "This is the temple of the Lord, the temple of the Lord, the temple of the Lord." (Jer. 7:3–4)

The loyalty which God desires involves freely chosen follow-through on commitment. No doubt it refers at one level to a style of life in community which is lacking in Israel. But context suggests that here loyalty is directed toward God as well as toward other people. In this passage the Yahweh-Israel relationship is more in view than the internal workings of the covenant people. What does it mean to suggest that dependent Israel might offer loyalty to Yahweh the suzerain? One clue lies in the verb used here, "to desire" or "to delight in" (Hebrew *hps*). The verb itself suggests that although Yahweh would take pleasure in the people's loyalty, there is no way to enforce or coerce their response. The previous verse suggests that the route of prophetic warning and divine discipline has not seemed to produce the desired loyalty in the people. Even though Yahweh remains powerful and Israel dependent, loyalty is still a quality which Israel is somehow free to offer or to withhold.[12] The only method of "enforcement" is divine judgment, which cannot in and of itself produce loyalty as *willing* commitment, even if it might get the people to act justly and remain faithful on a basis of fear. Hosea's unusual use of the Hebrew word for loyalty provides a way to speak of Israel's freedom even within the vassal relationship.

Part of the power of any poetry, and certainly of the poetry of biblical prophecy, lies in such using of familiar words in unfamiliar ways. The strange or grating usage holds in itself the power to bring an explosion of new insight to the hearer/reader. It opens the imagination, sets existence in a new perspective. So it is with Hosea and loyalty. The concept maintains its basic meaning in respect to communal life, yet a new and "impossible" dimension is added: God desires loyalty from Israel. This transformation of perception is aided by several additional clues within the contexts which speak of loyalty. Besides the verb "to delight in" of 6:6, Hosea's use of the word "faithfulness" and his recurrent emphasis on "knowledge of God," as well as his daring use of marriage imagery, contribute to this new understanding of loyalty.

## LOYALTY, KNOWLEDGE, AND FAITHFULNESS

Chapter 4 of Hosea marks the beginning of the second main

section of the book. It opens with another variation on the covenant lawsuit in the Mosaic covenant tradition:

> Hear the word of the Lord, O people of Israel;
>     for the Lord has a controversy with the inhabitants of
>     the land.
> There is no faithfulness or loyalty,
>     and no knowledge of God in the land;
> there is swearing, lying, killing, stealing, and committing
>     adultery;
>     they break all bounds and murder follows murder.
> Therefore the land mourns,
>     and all who dwell in it languish.
>
>                                        (Hos. 4:1–3a)

Yahweh states the case against Israel succinctly: faithfulness, loyalty, and knowledge of God are absent; the consequence is a life of communal disorder stemming from disobedience to divine command. Hosea's catalogue of forbidden dealings with neighbors is clearly reminiscent of the Ten Commandments, although the Hebrew verbs used are not identical in every case.[13] Although Hosea is most remembered for his criticism of Israel's religious syncretism, this passage makes clear his concern for issues of communal righteousness. But the two categories of worship and justice are not really separable in Hosea's view. Faithfulness, loyalty, and knowledge of God are missing because of syncretism; and it is their absence which leads to violation of the other commandments of the Decalogue.

Knowledge of God is a central concept for Hosea, as its final and climactic position in both 4:2 and 6:6 would suggest,[14] and it has several levels of meaning in his prophecy. It means, in the first place, knowledge of God's will as revealed in law. In the section of chap. 4 immediately following the lawsuit, the priests are castigated for their failure to communicate knowledge, which is specified as God's law:

> My people are destroyed for lack of knowledge;
>     because you have rejected knowledge,
>     I reject you from being a priest to me.

> And since you have forgotten the law of your God,
> I also will forget your children.
>
> (Hos. 4:6)

But this missing knowledge of "law" (Hebrew *torah*) means that far more than the commandments of the Sinai covenant has been forgotten. In fact, it is the whole story of Yahweh's dealings with the people—exodus as well as Sinai—which has been forgotten, laid aside or amalgamated with Canaanite religion. Because the people do not know the history of Yahweh's saving acts, they cannot recognize the true source of their present blessings:

> And she did not know
>     that it was I who gave her
>     the grain, the wine, and the oil,
> and who lavished upon her silver
>     and gold which they used for Baal.
>
> (Hos. 2:8)

Beyond such informational knowledge of tradition and commandment, knowledge of God is also a phrase that refers to relationships. Hosea's usage evokes the well-documented political use of the verb "to know" in the diplomacy of the ancient Near East. A vassal "knew" his suzerain in the sense of acknowledging him as his overlord; in the same way the suzerain "knew" his vassal, i.e., recognized the relationship as one he was committed to defend.[15] This relational nuance of knowing can be seen in the people's litany:

> Let us know, let us press on to know the Lord.
>
> (Hos. 6:3)

And it can be seen in the people's cry which God also rejects as false:

> My God, we Israel know thee.
>
> (Hos. 8:2)

Likewise Yahweh says to Israel:

> It was I who knew you in the wilderness,
>     in the land of drought;

but when they had fed to the full,
they were filled, and their heart was lifted up;
therefore they forgot me.
(Hos. 13:5-6)

Relational knowledge is not limited to the political sphere, however; knowledge also refers to the intimacy of partnership, including sexuality, of the marriage relationship. Hosea is at his boldest as he associates knowledge with marriage intimacy. A most fundamental contrast between Yahweh and deities of neighboring peoples was that Yahweh had no consort. "Yahweh alone is God" meant Yahweh alone. Religious rites in which human beings enacted the sexual relations of deities in order to ensure fertility had no place in pristine Yahweh worship. In Hosea's time, this theology had been compromised by syncretism. Altars had been built to other gods (8:11; 10:1), and sacred prostitution had been introduced (4:13b-14). The prophet, in the face of this situation, uses (of all things!) the metaphor of a marriage relationship as a primary image for conveying the brokenness of the covenant between Yahweh and Israel. Since "knowledge" is part of marriage vocabulary, texts that reflect the suzerain-vassal metaphor carry the overtone of the marriage imagery as well. The contrast between God's knowledge of Israel and Israel's lack of knowledge of God is explicitly connected to Israel's marriage infidelity (harlotry) in a passage that also plays on the idea of God's "knowing" as not being fooled or hoodwinked:

I know Ephraim,
and Israel is not hid from me;
for now, O Ephraim, you have played the harlot,
Israel is defiled.
Their deeds do not permit them
to return to their God.
For the spirit of harlotry is within them,
and they know not the Lord.
(Hos. 5:3-4)

In sum, Hosea works theologically with the whole range of the Hebrew word "knowledge." From information about commandment and saving history, to the covenant image of the suzerain-vassal relationship, to the discernment of truth and the riskier metaphor of marriage intimacy, he uses and reuses a word that can draw together the chief emphases of his message.

Hosea's concept of knowledge of God has been developed here at some length because it can help to clarify his special twist on loyalty. We have seen that the two concepts occur together both in his proclamation of what is lacking in Israel (4:1) and in his summation of what God desires from the people (6:6). Hosea brings the terms together yet a third time in his new covenant picture of the eschatological future (2:19–20; see below, "The Gift of Loyalty"), again with knowledge of God in the climactic concluding position.

Knowledge is different from loyalty in that in normal Hebrew usage knowledge can be bidirectional. The suzerain may recognize the vassal, as well as the vassal the suzerain. Intimate marriage knowledge refers to both members of the relationship.[16] Each party may have information about the other. Thus the question of who is the weaker or the more powerful, who is in distress and who is able to rescue, does not figure directly in the use of the verb "to know," even though those involved may participate in a very unequal relationship. This bidirectionality is one clue to Hosea's transformation of the idea of loyalty. Loyalty that was a one-directional word, applied only from God to Israel, is now deliberately turned around. Placing the word back to back with a bidirectional term helps the hearer to grasp the change. Loyalty as faithful living out of the commandments concerning the neighbor would not simply be obedience by a series of individuals. If the commandments were carried out by the community as a whole, then the community as an entity would be showing loyalty to God.

Another clue to Hosea's different emphasis in speaking of loyalty lies in the word "faithfulness," which appears in 4:1. The meaning of the word pair "loyalty and faithfulness" has been discussed in chapter 2, "Stories of Human Loyalty," and in chapter 3, "Freedom and Commitment." Here it is important to recognize that the term "faithfulness" used independently is, like "knowledge," a bidirectional term. Although the word appears only in 4:1 in Hosea,[17] other Old Testament usage suggests that Israel could serve God in faithfulness (Josh. 24:14; 1 Sam. 12:24; cf. 2 Kings 20:3), despite the rarity of such usage compared to God's faithfulness to Israel. When Hosea comes to use this word pair, he draws special attention to his unusual usage of "loyalty" by reversing the fixed order of the pair: he says "faithfulness and loyalty," in contrast to normal usage.[18] Again a literary device puts the hearer/ reader on notice that a special nuance of loyalty is being developed. Here the reversed word pair brings "loyalty" close to our general English sense of unswerving attachment, persevering commitment, without regard to status within the relationship.

It is noteworthy that both Joshua 24 and 1 Samuel 12 speak of Israel's faithfulness to Yahweh specifically in contrast to the possibility of religious apostasy, serving other gods. The theme of choice and not turning back dominates the covenant at Shechem in Joshua 24; Samuel's farewell speech urges the Israelites not to "turn aside after vain things which cannot profit or save" (1 Sam. 12:21). This usage suggests that the contrast between faithfulness and syncretistic apostasy is intended in Hosea 4 also. Lack of faithfulness, loyalty, and knowledge is not, for Hosea, simply synonymous with disruption of the internal fabric of the covenant community. More than that, the lack of these three elements means lack of right relationship with Yahweh, of which lying, stealing, murdering, and the rest are the symptom and inevitable consequence.

## LOYALTY AND THE
## MARRIAGE METAPHOR

This new view of loyalty as something that Israel could (but fails to) offer to God is furthered by the overall marriage imagery used in Hosea, to which the concept of knowledge contributes in part. Since marriage was patriarchally structured in ancient Israel, the imagery is one-sided: God the husband is pictured as in power and in the right, Israel the wife is subordinate and in the wrong for violating marriage vows. Despite the serious difficulties with the use of such imagery in our contemporary culture,[19] there was a personal dimension of the ancient marriage relationship which does still ring true and which Hosea uses in support of his new perspective on loyalty. In time of crisis, either husband or wife could show loyalty to the other; need rather than role informed the concept of loyalty. The story of Sarah and Abraham, discussed in chapter 2, "Stories of Human Loyalty," illustrates the extent to which a wife might go to show loyalty to her husband. To preserve her husband's life Sarah pretended they were not married, even at the cost of being taken into Abimelech's harem. Here in Hosea, Israel the wife has gone quite the opposite way. In a deluded effort to improve her own lot she has become an adulteress and indeed has even lived as a harlot, taking many lovers (Canaanite deities) in expectation of being paid (with improved crops and the like). The image runs through much of the book but is especially striking in the following passages:

> Plead with your mother, plead—
> > for she is not my wife,
> > and I am not her husband—
> that she put away her harlotry from her face,
> > and her adultery from between her breasts;
>
> . . . . . . . . . . . . . . . .
>
> For their mother has played the harlot;
> > she that conceived them has acted shamefully.
> For she said, "I will go after my lovers,
> > who give me my bread and my water,
> > my wool and my flax, my oil and my drink."
> > > > (Hos. 2:2, 5)

And the Lord said to me, "Go again, love a woman who is beloved of a paramour and is an adulteress; even as the Lord loves the people of Israel, though they turn to other gods and love cakes of raisins." (Hos. 3:1)

> They shall eat, but not be satisfied;
> > they shall play the harlot, but not multiply;
> because they have forsaken the Lord
> > to cherish harlotry.
> > > > (Hos. 4:10)

Loyalty calls for sticking by a relationship, cherishing it even when times are not so good; Israel, forgetting all Yahweh's benefits, has betrayed the intimacy of their relationship to "cherish harlotry"

(4:10). Loyalty that is like the morning dew (6:4) is no loyalty at all (4:1).

Jeremiah, in a section which suggests that his early prophecy may have been especially informed by traditions from Hosea, makes this same point:

> Thus says the Lord,
>   I remember the loyalty of your youth,
>     your love as a bride,
>   how you followed me in the wilderness,
>     in a land not sown.
>
>                    (Jer. 2:2)

This recollection of the earliest days of Yahweh's covenant with Israel, when the community held close to God,[20] stands as a kind of backdrop against which Jeremiah develops a whole variety of descriptions of the people's subsequent apostasy. Although the word "loyalty" does not appear again after this opening verse, it functions as the contrastive term for the many references to Israel's harlotry which follow in Jeremiah 2—3. The poem that immediately follows these lines in 2:4–13 once again uses the covenant lawsuit form to depict Israel's failure of loyalty; and the harlotry theme serves shockingly to dramatize and personalize the covenant breaking:

> Yea, upon every high hill
>   and under every green tree
>   you bowed down as a harlot.
>                    (Jer. 2:20b)

> Can a maiden forget her ornaments,
>   or a bride her attire?
> Yet my people have forgotten me
>   days without number.
>                    (Jer. 2:32)

> You have played the harlot with many lovers;
>   and would you return to me?
>                         says the Lord.
> Lift up your eyes to the bare heights, and see!
>   Where have you not been lain with?
>                    (Jer. 3:1c–2a)

> Surely, as a faithless wife leaves her husband,
> so have you been faithless to me, O house of Israel,
> says the Lord.
> (Jer. 3:20)

In these two chapters Jeremiah has almost nothing to say about specific matters of justice within the Israelite community, although he develops such themes elsewhere. Only a little is said condemning international alliances, which Hosea also treats under the metaphor of marital infidelity. Rather, Jeremiah's focus here is directly upon Israel's religious apostasy, the turning to gods "as many as your cities" (2:28) who are "no gods" and "do not profit" (2:11).[21] Thus the entire section centers in on the "vertical" dimension of the relationship between Yahweh and the people.

In the picture of original fidelity in Jer. 2:2, it is completely clear that Israel's loyalty was directed toward Yahweh. Unlike some of the Hosea texts where communal righteousness remains in view, here in Jeremiah's context of the marriage metaphor loyalty is clearly broken loose from its powerful-to-weak moorings, as the intracommunal aspect recedes into the background. The future of the marriage relationship depended upon Israel's ways, and in those early times all went well. Here loyalty does not consist of a single identifiable act; it is, in effect, contrasted with the dramatically nonloyal acts of apostasy. But the implication is that the Yahweh relationship is a way of life which must be worked at, that a life style for Israel loyal to Yahweh would be the composite of all those acts of worship and service which in their very doing would have kept the community close to God.

The metaphor of marriage thus reinforces the bidirectional use of faithfulness and knowledge in Israel's religious tradition and presses toward a bidirectional understanding of loyalty as well. The incoercible character of acts of loyalty undergirds this shift, so that Hosea especially and later Jeremiah mold a new understanding of loyalty in which Israel is incredibly expected and invited to offer loyalty to Yahweh. The loyalty expected is clearly directed toward the coming into being of a *shalom* community. But a *shalom* community means not only observance of the second table of the Decalogue concerning neighbors, as emphasized in Micah 6, but also the first table concerning sole allegiance to God, as is suggested most clearly in Hosea 6 and Jeremiah 2. Thus loyalty moves beyond general humanitarian concern to become a "charged" word in which is caught up the entire Decalogue, indeed everything of the spirit, not only the letter, of Israel's relationship to Yahweh.

## THE ANGUISH OF GOD

Hosea's unusual interpretation of loyalty offers new insight not only concerning Israel but concerning Yahweh as well. The marriage image in particular invites the portrayal of a whole range of emotion on the part of the divine husband. Abraham Heschel has emphasized the importance of divine emotion as opposed to neutrality in all of Hebrew prophecy:

> Prophecy is the voice that God has lent to the silent agony, a voice to the plundered poor. . . . God is raging in the prophet's words.[22]

The "divine pathos," which takes shape in love or in anger, is evoked by behavior of the covenant community. Thus humanity is "relevant to God" in the prophetic perspective; God is not impassible but is affected by what goes on in the world.[23]

The one aspect of loyalty that is most difficult to appropriate in Hosea's reversal of the usual direction of God to Israel is that of helper to the needy, the situationally powerful to situationally dependent. But precisely by using loyalty in such a gratingly impossible way of Israel toward God, Hosea lifts up before his hearers the pathos of God, the deep yearning of God for the people's response, the relevance to God of their response. The divine initiative and pleading echo with a mix of love, anger, and frustration which eddy and swirl in expression of the anguish of God. Nowhere is this anguish clearer than in the marriage imagery of the violation of intimacy:

> Plead with your mother, plead—
>     for she is not my wife,
>     and I am not her husband—
> that she put away her harlotry from her face,
>     and her adultery from between her breasts.
>                             (Hos. 2:2)

> Now I will uncover her lewdness
>> in the sight of her lovers,
>> and no one shall rescue her out of my hand.
> And I will put an end to all her mirth,
>> her feasts, her new moons, her sabbaths,
>> and all her appointed feasts.
>> (Hos. 2:10–11)

This same deep pain of God is expressed also in Hosea's metaphor of parent[24] and child:

> When Israel was a child, I loved him,
>> and out of Egypt I called my son.
> The more I called them,
>> the more they went from me.
>
> . . . . . . . . . . . . .
>
> They shall return to the land of Egypt,
>> and Assyria shall be their king,
>> because they have refused to return to me.
>
> . . . . . . . . . . . . . . . . . .
>
> How can I give you up, O Ephraim!
> How can I hand you over, O Israel!
>
> . . . . . . . . . . . . . . . . .
>
> My heart recoils within me,
>> my compassion grows warm and tender.
>> (Hos. 11:1–2a, 5, 8a and c)

Within this framework of God's anguish, each reference to Israel's failure to show loyalty reiterates the frustration of the divine partner who has staked everything on Israel's willingness to respond, only to realize that the response simply is not forthcoming:

> I would redeem them,
>> but they speak lies against me.
>> (Hos. 7:13b)

> Were I to write for him my laws by ten thousands,
>> they would be regarded as a strange thing.
>> (Hos. 8:12)

Religious apostasy, wholesale abandonment of concern for neighbor, murder and intrigue in high places, entangling international alliances—all that Hosea sees about him testifies to covenant breaking and unfaithfulness. Despite all of Yahweh's efforts through the prophets and through chastisement, Israel's loyalty remains at best "like the morning dew."

EXHORTATION TO LOYALTY

Israel's recalcitrance would seem to be irreversible. Yet Yahweh does not give up. Hosea still issues specific exhortations to change of life style; two of these are set forth as calls to loyalty. Again anticipating the themes of Micah 6, he urges the people to repent:

> So you, by the help of your God, return,
>    hold fast to loyalty and justice,
>    and wait continually for your God.
>                                    (Hos. 12:6)

The lines appear within material concerning the Jacob tradition, a notoriously difficult section of the book, and their relationship to context is not very clear. Hans Walter Wolff's interpretation is plausible: these words specify what God said to Jacob at Bethel (cf. v. 4c), and Israel is urged to follow the example of the patriarch who sought God's favor.[25]

Here, as in Mic. 6:8, the themes of loyalty and justice are brought together, conveying the importance of legal recourse accessible to all and legal decisions made without favoritism or prejudice because of societal status. Justice truly lived out in community manifests the spirit of loyalty; such a community would find itself by definition moving toward life in accord with Yahweh, who loves justice.

The exhortation to "wait continually for your God" reinforces the sense of the verb "to hold fast" of the previous line and sets the hoped-for life style of Israel in contrast to that pictured in 4:2 and 6:4. There the absence of loyalty means covenant breaking run rampant, with leadership so far from the ways of God that no hope for real change is in sight. Even in any effort to change, loyalty is evanescent and repentance quickly withers. "To hold fast" and "to wait continually" lift up the quality of permanence as basic to any genuine return; only by "the help of God"[26] might such a change take place. At the same time, the expressions "to hold fast" and especially "to wait continually" focus attention on the durative aspect of loyalty and on its vertical dimensions. Waiting continually for God describes what Israel's loyalty to God would look like; and such waiting would overflow in a life style of loyalty in community. Like Micah's call to "walk humbly," so Hosea's call to "wait continually" epitomizes the essence of loyal covenant living.

In the larger setting of Hosea 12, it appears that Hosea's exhortation is really expected to fall upon deaf ears, however, for he turns immediately to illustrating Ephraim's unchecked and unabashed unjust dealings:

> A trader, in whose hands are false balances,
>     he loves to oppress.
>
> (Hos. 12:7)

It is almost as if the call to repentance is included as a foil to reveal the hopelessness of Israel's situation because of the people's inability to respond.

This same pattern of exhortation followed by renewed indictment appears also in Hos. 10:12–13. Using farming and nature imagery, the prophet calls for a different life style:

> Sow for yourselves what partakes of righteousness
>     and you shall reap in accordance with loyalty;
> break up your fallow ground,
>     for it is time to seek Yahweh,
>     that he may come and make salvation rain upon you.
> You have cultivated wickedness,
>     you have reaped injustice,
>     you have eaten the fruit of falsehood.
>
> (Hos. 10:12–13a, au. trans.)

In whatever way the complex grammatical and textual difficulties of v. 13 are resolved, the point is that divine salvation will follow upon Israel's righteousness and loyalty. Israel is not to reap loyalty from Yahweh, but to reap what comes from its own loyalty.[27]

In the poetic pairing of righteousness and loyalty of v. 12, Hosea moves a step beyond the pairing with justice of 12:6. It is widely recognized, following Gerhard von Rad and the much earlier work of H. Cremer,[28] that righteousness in the Old Testament does not refer to some abstract ethical standard. Rather, righteousness has to do with living and acting in a way appropriate to a relationship. For individuals, righteousness is a function of their many and changing interconnections with others; for the community as a whole, the word also provides a way of speaking of the entire fabric of the society itself, its warp and woof. The concept of justice (Hebrew *mishpāṭ*), discussed in connection with Micah 6 and Hosea 12, is integral to righteousness (Hebrew *ṣĕdāqâ*) in that justice is especially concerned for the mechanisms by which righteousness is maintained in community. Righteousness is the broader and more radical concept. Thus our English word "justice" in a sense covers both Hebrew concepts in the different nuances of the English term: if there is "justice" within the court system (*mishpāṭ*), it will undergird and help to bring about a society characterized by "justice" (*ṣĕdāqâ*).

The call for loyalty in connection with righteousness points to that aspect of righteousness which is most difficult to achieve. So long as life goes smoothly and there are few hard choices to be made, righteousness is not so difficult to live out, before God and with people round about. But life is more often filled with situations in which, individually or communally, it is (or seems) easier to "cultivate wickedness." Hosea confronts Israel at such a time. Political uncertainty was yielding assassinations (6:9), subversive internal and international alliances (7:6–10), and futile military buildup (10:13b); economic uncertainty was yielding greedy manipulation; religious confusion was yielding syncretism (4:4–10; 13:1–2; etc.). When righteousness proves difficult, when it is easier just to let the situation drift along toward destruction, then it is that loyalty comes into play. Loyalty means taking the obligations of all relationships (personal or communal) seriously, even those it would be easy and convenient to ignore, those where the need is great and no repayment is foreseeable. Loyalty means putting another person or group or even the whole world at greater value than oneself. Loyalty means seeking Yahweh alone even though Baal worship looks like good insurance and "everybody's doing it." Loyalty is that attitude which enables one to say no to injustice (unrighteousness); loyalty is every action, small or great, which embodies that no.

Yahweh invites Israel to show loyalty and reap its fruit—the salvation[29] of God. But Yahweh does not see much hope for such a change by the people. Their past record of wickedness and injustice is recalled immediately in 10:13 and then illustrated in the following verses by their present behavior. The immediate context of the exhortation anticipates nothing but annihilation of the unjust, unknowing, unfaithful, unrighteous, and disloyal people of God.

## THE GIFT OF LOYALTY

But the One who declares, "I will destroy you, O Israel; who can help you?" (Hos. 13:9) is also the One who asks, "How can I give you up, O Ephraim!" (11:8) and who declares, "I am divine, not human" (11:9). It is this same Yahweh who offers beyond the judgment "a door of hope" (2:15). In a picture of eschatological restoration, Hosea presents Yahweh's new salvific initiative by playing with the marriage metaphor in 2:14–20.

The section begins with a wilderness setting in which Yahweh will "allure" Israel and "speak tenderly to her" (2:14). The language evokes the image of wooing and even sexual intimacy, again typical of Hosea's bold use of the Canaanite imagery against itself. The picture of the bride is reinforced by our awareness of Jeremiah's later reference to the original wilderness period as the time of Israel's bridal loyalty.

In the next verses, marriage imagery is treated in another way; it is developed in a word play designed to show the rejection of Baalism:

> And in that day, says the Lord, you will call me, "My husband," and no longer will you call me, "My Baal." For I will remove the names of the Baals from her mouth, and they shall be mentioned by name no more. (Hos. 2:16–17)

The proper name Baal when used as a common noun meant lord or owner and was used as a word for husband.[30] The rejection of this title may serve to lift up the personal over the legal dimensions of Israel's future relationship to God.[31] But more important is the symbolization of the end of confusion between Yahweh and the gods of Canaanite religion. Worship will be reformed, and adultery (harlotry) will come to an end.

The divine establishment of a (new) covenant in which all nature will join and through which peace will reign (2:18) is given specificity for Israel in terms of yet a third and climactic play on the marriage image:

> And I will betroth you to me for ever; and I will betroth you to me with [a bride price of] righteousness and justice and loyalty and mercy; and I will betroth you to me with [a bride price of] faithfulness; and you shall know Yahweh. (Hos. 2:19–20, au. trans.)

Here Yahweh is pictured making the final arrangements for marriage by stating what will be paid to the father of the bride, except of course that in this case the gifts are really for Israel itself as the bride.

It is not self-evident that the qualities listed are those which Israel itself will manifest, rather than qualities which Yahweh will display toward the people. But to take seriously the imagery of betrothal gifts suggests that they do come into the "possession" of the bride's family. Furthermore, the betrothal gifts catalogued here are precisely those qualities which the Israel of Hosea's time is lacking, according to the rest of his prophecy; loyalty, faithfulness,[32] and knowledge are lacking in the land (4:1); loyalty and knowledge are desired by God (6:6); loyalty and justice would be characteristic of repentance (12:6); loyalty and righteousness should be sown by Israel (10:12). Only the word "mercy" in the series is new; its inclusion may be influenced by the motif of the child named "Not pitied" (or "No mercy") in 1:6 and finally shown pity in the reversal of the children's names in 2:22–23. The community that in the end receives mercy will "on that day" be enabled also to show mercy.

Recognizing that the people is so enmeshed in its sin that it is indeed unable to repent, that its loyalty cannot but be fickle, God proposes to bring about a new thing in the earth. All those qualities which make for *shalom,* all which are so miserably lacking in the community, Yahweh will simply give to them. They will not have to conjure them up by an act of their own will. In

Jeremiah's way of putting it, the law (*torah*) will be written on their hearts, so that all will "know the Lord" without having to be taught (Jer. 31:31–34).

And so from Hosea's perspective it is clear that loyalty, like those other qualities which loyalty undergirds when they seem easier to ignore, can never be achieved solely by human effort. God castigates the people for their failure of loyalty and announces judgment. Obviously their efforts at loyalty are insufficient. But also, judgment alone is insufficient to turn the community around. A new initiative of divine loyalty is needed in which it is finally Yahweh who brings in the reign of God, not the people by themselves or in their own power.

Because love outlives wrath in the pathos of God, loyalty will blossom at last in Israel. In that community where loyalty is loved and held fast, righteousness will flourish and justice will be done for all. There will be concern for the least ones, and that concern will not fade or wither. The people will keep the Decalogue (show loyalty) as their purified relationship to Yahweh overflows in a just and righteous communal life. They shall indeed know Yahweh. And because Yahweh will bring it about "for ever" (Hos. 2:19), the Holy One need no longer "withdraw" (5:6; cf. Exodus 33) but can truly be the One in the midst of the people, the One who "will not come to destroy" (11:9). Out of God's unimaginably great loyalty, ultimately surprising in its offer of covenant renewal, will come something even more surprising and unimagined, a human community characterized by that same loyalty.

LOYALTY IN THE INTERIM

Loyalty as a fully realized community life style lies in the eschatological future. But what about loyalty in the meantime? . . . Although the Old Testament focuses primarily on relationship between God and the people as community, and although individual identity was closely bound up with community in ancient Israel, nonetheless loyalty was recognized as a quality which some people manifested more than others. Loyalty was praiseworthy; there was expectation that it would be honored by God.

The individual who manifested loyalty was sometimes referred to as a *ḥāsîd*,[33] although the word seems originally to have referred to a *recipient* of divine loyalty. In some places the plural is preserved in this latter sense and is used to include the whole people of Israel:

> He has raised up a horn for his people,
>     praise for all his saints [*ḥasidim*],
>     for the people of Israel who are near to him.
> (Ps. 148:14)

But even in this example, the faithfulness of the people may be as much in view as is their experience of God's loyalty.

Other texts more clearly single out the upright as belonging to this category of people described as loyal:

> Depart from evil, and do good;
>     so shall you abide for ever.
> For the Lord loves justice;
>     he will not forsake his loyal ones.
> (Ps. 37:27–28)

Since this psalm repeatedly contrasts those who trust God and live righteously over against the wicked who will be cut off and perish, the loyal ones here should be equated with the righteous, with those who do good.

Micah laments the demise of the "godly" (RSV):

> The loyal one has perished from the earth,
>     and not one human being is upright;
> all of them lie in wait for blood,
>     they hunt one another with nets.
> (Mic. 7:2, au. trans.)

The passage continues with a devastating picture of a land devoid of those who manifest loyalty, stripped of any who live before Yahweh and neighbor with steadfastness, commitment, and concern for others rather than self. Instead, everyone does evil diligently and perverts justice when the opportunity arises (v. 3). In such a time even one's own relatives cannot be trusted (vv. 5–6); the speaker can look only to Yahweh for salvation (v. 7). By implication, of course, the speaker of Mic. 7:1–7 is the loyal one whose refusal to turn aside to evil has brought only loneliness and trouble.

A few times the word "loyalty" is used in the plural to refer to the good works of the devout person.[34] Hezekiah and Josiah were remembered as the two kings of Judah who followed most closely the will of Yahweh and the heritage of their ancestor David, and the Chronicler concludes his reports of their respective reigns in the following words:

> Now the rest of the acts of Hezekiah, and his loyal deeds, behold, they are written . . . in the Book of the Kings of Judah and Israel. (2 Chron. 32:32)

> Now the rest of the acts of Josiah, and his loyal deeds according to what is written in the law of the Lord, and his acts, first and last, behold, they are written in the Book of the Kings of Israel and Judah. (2 Chron. 35:26–27)

The second text specifies the meaning of loyal deeds as obedience to divine law. This sense is congruent with Hosea's interpretation of loyalty as observance of the Decalogue demand for faithfulness to God and neighbor. Hosea's concern was to show that such loyalty was lacking in Israel's community life style. In the Chronicler the emphasis has moved toward an enumeration of loyal acts which enable the recognition of individuals who have lived faithfully before God. Loyal living represents piety in the best and most positive sense of the word: devotion to God and active pursuit of justice and righteousness in the life of the community.

Near the conclusion of his memoirs, Nehemiah reports that the temple Levites had left their duties because their supporting allowances had been cut off. He called them back and reestablished tithing in all Judah to provide for them. He then adds, before turning to his other accomplishments:

> Remember me, O my God, concerning this, and wipe not out my loyal deeds that I have done for the house of my God and for his service. (Neh. 13:14)

It is possible that the term "loyalty" in this text and the previous two focused especially upon the support of correct temple worship; for Hezekiah and Josiah were most noted for their reform and purification of the Jerusalem cult, and Nehemiah's petition is found in a similar context. The authors of these materials clearly had a particular interest in all things related to temple observance. Given their context in the Persian period when many Jews even in Jerusalem were losing touch with their religious roots and lively faith, this emphasis may well have reflected the critical illustration of loyalty in their time.

Whether loyalty is viewed in this rather narrow context of worship, or whether taken in the broader setting of walking with discernment by upholding all the divine instruction, the characterization of the God-fearing or pious individual as loyal "belongs to a time when personal loyalty to YHWH has become an explicit and self-conscious issue."[35] This notion of self-conscious personal loyalty to Yahweh brings our study of human loyalty full circle. All the examples of individual loyalty that were reviewed in chapter 2, "Stories of Human Loyalty," were indeed "secular" in the sense that the word "loyalty" was used of people's actions in the usual course of everyday living. Those people were not being asked to do a special "religious" act. Nevertheless, insofar as loyalty encompasses the whole of the life of faith, all acts furthering justice and righteousness, and especially any acts in which God's care for all people is lived out in human support for another individual or group in need, then all those acts of David and Ruth and Rahab and Joseph and the others must be seen as small windows onto the loyal life style which God so earnestly desires.

The critical phrase is "God's care." Sometimes acts that are loyal from a human point of view may run counter to God's care; situations of uncertainty call for difficult choices, and self-delusion is all too easy. Loyalty humanly conceived can represent failure of loyalty from the divine perspective. But by the same token, the most ordinary act of caring, done without any special thought of religious import, contributes its part to a loyal life style of faithfulness in action.

This discussion of loyalty in the interim cannot conclude, however, without a reminder: Israel's interest in personal good deeds manifesting loyalty never erased its concern for communal loyalty in which the justice of God might be realized in a fuller way. Israel would have been puzzled by our modern debate over whether social reform must begin with conversion of the individual or pressure on the social structure. If the issue could have been grasped, the answer in ancient Israel would surely have been "both/and," for individual and community were not seen in such a dichotomy. Loyalty as personal good works and loyalty as communal commitment to the weak of society were two sides of a single coin. The individual's works of loyalty needed ever to be directed toward bringing the whole people closer to God's way; the communal concern, although it was more often fleeting than steadfast, was directed toward offering life—space, place, peace, justice—to the least individual. So it is that the answer given to the individual questioner of Micah 6 speaks in the same breath to the very heart of the whole community of faith:

> And what does Yahweh ask of you
> but to do justice, and to love loyalty,
> and to walk attentively with your God?
> (Mic. 6:8, au. trans.)

### NOTES

1. James L. Mays, *Micah*, OTL (Philadelphia: Westminster Press, 1976), 137. Mays argues convincingly that Mic. 6:6–8 forms a unit form-critically independent of 6:1–5. The important thematic connection to 6:1–5 seen by H. Huffmon ("The Covenant Lawsuit in the Prophets," *JBL* 78 [1959]:285–95) and J. Harvey (*Le plaidoyer prophétique contre Israël après la rupture de l'alliance* [Montréal: Les Éditions Bellarmin, 1967]) is not imagined, but results from editorial joining of the two units.

2. Mays, *Micah*, 136.

3. The expression "people of God" is chosen for its pregnant ambiguity. Probably Micah has first in mind the "covenant community" in the narrower sense of seeking loyal living on Israel's "home front." But even Israel's law showed concern for "resident aliens." And Mic. 6:8 does not state any restriction on justice and loyalty. Just as the intended recipients of loyalty may be identified as all humanity, not only covenant people, so also the expression "people of God" may be construed in this broad sense as well as in the narrower one.

4. For a provocative exposition of this theme, see Walter Brueggemann, *Living Toward a Vision: Biblical Reflections on Shalom* (Philadel-

phia: United Church Press, 1976), esp. 95–112. "In a *shalom* community," he writes, "the king listens to the prophet and cares for the poor, because that is his office; the prophet speaks boldly and constructively, because he knows the king intends to rule well; the powerless are coming to power" (p. 100).

5. I think of Jesus' suggestion to invite the poor to one's banquet, not the rich neighbors, "lest they also invite you in return, and you be repaid" (Luke 14:12–14).

6. Mays, *Micah*, 142.

7. It seems likely that the word "man" in Mic. 6:8 really meant males in the first instance, since males owned the property which could be given for sacrifice, males were the predominant participants in worship, and males were inducted into the covenant community. Yet the prophet, if asked, would presumably have agreed that women should love loyalty also.

8. Exodus, wilderness, Transjordan, and taking of the land ("from Shittim to Gilgal") are traditional and paradigmatic as a summary for all divine blessing.

9. Cf. Harvey, *Le plaidoyer prophétique*.

10. Some of the texts are grammatically or exegetically ambiguous. Detailed arguments for each disputed instance can be found in my *The Meaning of Hesed in the Hebrew Bible*, HSM 17 (Missoula, Mont.: Scholars Press, 1978), 170–88.

11. For a discussion of this issue, see James L. Mays, *Hosea*, OTL (Philadelphia: Westminster Press, 1969), 93–96; also Hans Walter Wolff, *Hosea*, Hermeneia (Philadelphia: Fortress Press, 1974), 117–19.

12. A similar case could be made for the verb "to require" (Hebrew *drš*, "to seek") in Mic. 6:8.

13. On the pattern of these verbs, see Francis I. Andersen and David Noel Freedman, *Hosea*, AB 24 (Garden City, N.Y.: Doubleday & Co., 1980), 336–39.

14. For a listing of Hosea's references to knowledge, see Mays, *Hosea*, 63–64.

15. H. B. Huffmon, "The Treaty Background of Hebrew Yāda'," *BASOR* 181 (1966):31–37.

16. Although in specific reference to sexual intercourse the male is regularly the subject of the verb.

17. Striking in its scarcity here, this word also, like loyalty, is not used of God in Hosea. The etymologically related term '*ĕmûnâ*, with essentially the same meaning, appears in 2:20. See below, in this chapter, "The Gift of Loyalty," 121–23.

18. The only other exception to the fixed order in the entire Old Testament occurs in Mic. 7:20. There the words are in parallel poetic

lines, not so closely positioned as here. Also peculiar there is the unusual order Jacob-Abraham for the patriarchs in the two lines. One wonders whether the lines themselves have been reversed, whether deliberately in composition or in the course of their transmission.

19. It is important to emphasize once again the danger of the abuse of this biblical metaphor when its one-sidedness is not properly recognized. Men are as likely as women to violate their marriage vows; wives are as likely as husbands to show extraordinary loyalty. Our cognitive awareness of this reality tends to be undercut by the evocative power of the biblical image of the faithless wife, carried on in the New Testament by the theme of the purified bride of Christ. See chap. 3, "Freedom and Commitment," 68 n. 44. Sallie McFague's discussion of the twin problems of the idolatry and irrelevance of religious language generally (*Metaphorical Theology: Models of God in Religious Language* [Philadelphia: Fortress Press, 1982], 4–9) and of patriarchal language in particular in the contemporary Christian context (pp. 145–51) may be applied to the metaphor of God the husband as well as to God the father which is her central focus.

20. The Old Testament tradition as a whole is not consistent with Jeremiah's view of the wilderness period as a time of fidelity. The Pentateuch pictures the era as one of repeated murmuring and rebellion; cf. Psalms 78; 106; Ezekiel 20. Given the strength of this rebellion tradition, Jeremiah's claim is truly remarkable. Possibly his point is that despite the murmuring, apostasy to other gods was not part of Israel's desert life. But how then would he have understood the golden calf? Since Amos even implied that there was no sacrifice in the wilderness (Amos 5:25), it is plausible to suggest differing traditions in Israel concerning this bygone but paradigmatic era.

21. The expression "do not profit" is among several that appear to be puns on the name of the god Baal of the Canaanite pantheon. See John Bright, *Jeremiah*, AB 21 (Garden City, N.Y.: Doubleday & Co., 1965), 15.

22. Abraham Heschel, *The Prophets: An Introduction* (New York: Harper & Row, 1962), 5.

23. Abraham Heschel, *The Prophets: Volume II* (New York: Harper & Row, 1962), chaps. 1—3, esp. pp. 9–11, 39–40. See also his excellent illustrative treatment of pathos in Hosea in *The Prophets: An Introduction*, 39–60.

24. The sex of the parent is not specified in the text; the activities of teaching to walk and bending down to feed would probably be thought of mainly as maternal in Israelite culture.

25. Wolff, *Hosea*, 213–14.

26. The grammatical structure of this line in Hebrew is extremely

130    FAITHFULNESS IN ACTION

unusual and its meaning is debated. However it is explained, most translations agree with the general sense suggested by the RSV.

27. The RSV "fruit of loyalty" (following the Greek) would still refer to
Israel's loyalty, since in this Hebrew construction the genitive always refers
to the plant which produces the fruit (e.g., "fruit *of the vine*"), never to the
name of the fruit itself.

28. H. Cremer, *Die paulinische Rechtfertigungslehre im Zusammenhang
ihrer geschichtlichen Voraussetzungen* (Gütersloh: Bertelsmann, 1901),
34ff.; Gerhard von Rad, *Old Testament Theology I* (New York: Harper &
Brothers, 1962), 375–83.

29. The Hebrew word for "salvation" in this text is identical to the word
for the "righteousness" which Israel is to sow. The repetition highlights the
interplay between the power of divine justice in the world and the need for
responsiveness in the human community.

30. E.g., Exod. 21:22. It should be noted that the other common word
for husband which Hosea announces as the replacement is simply the
word for "man," used as in the old English expression "man and wife."

31. So Wolff, *Hosea*, 49. But the evidence comes only from third
person usage, not direct address of wife to husband.

32. The Hebrew noun is *'ĕmûnâ* in Hosea 2, *'ĕmet* in Hosea 4; the two
come from the same root and function synonymously.

33. A modern derivative from this word, "hasidic" Judaism, will be
familiar to many. The RSV often translates the plural as "saints," sometimes as "faithful (ones)." Most Old Testament occurrences are in the
psalms.

34. The plural form of the word appears mostly in psalms and nearly
always refers to Yahweh's loyalty (either as an "intensive" use of the plural
[synonymous with great loyalty] or implying God's many individual acts of
loyalty). The usage for human piety may be a postexilic linguistic development or a restricted nuance, since it appears only in Nehemiah and
Chronicles.

35. Mays, *Micah*, 151.

CHAPTER 6

# Review and Reflection:
# Loyalty in
# Biblical Life Style

## RECAPITULATION

The preceding chapters have traced the characteristic features of
the Old Testament conception of loyalty in its divine/human and
corporate/individual polarities. The basic meaning of loyalty, most
generally described, has been seen to include the following:

— Loyalty is to another person (or persons) in relationship with
the one who acts loyally; loyalty is not to an idea or a cause.
— Loyalty is attitude made manifest in concrete action.
— Loyalty is offered to a person in need by a person who has
the ability to help; often only one person is in a position to
fill the need. Narrative texts tend to focus on dramatic
needs, but even the smallest need in the most everyday
situation might become an occasion for showing loyalty,
insofar as the fulfilling of the need is significant for the
vitality of the relationship.
— The need places the potential recipient in a position of
dependence on the one who may show loyalty.
— There are no societal legal sanctions for the failure to show
loyalty; thus the doer is in a situation of free decision.
— Hence, loyalty is shown in a freely undertaken carrying
through of an existing commitment to another who is now in
a situation of need.

This bulky and awkward last sentence attempts to capture the
principal nuances of the Hebrew term *ḥesed*. But any wooden
adoption of this sentence as though it provided a tight definition

131

would be simplistic and would do injustice to the variety of emphases found in different parts of the Old Testament.

God's relationship to Israel was expressed in the Old Testament primarily under a covenant metaphor. Divine loyalty within covenant involved both God's commitment to Israel and the ever new free decision of God to continue to honor that commitment by preserving and supporting the covenant community. Divine freedom and divine self-obligation were held together in this single word, which expressed also God's strength and Israel's need for divine care.

The Sinai covenant in its strict theoretical form presupposed that Israel's sin would lead to the end of the covenant relationship. The depth of Yahweh's loyalty was revealed in repeated decisions to forgive apostasy and injustice. Yet such forgiveness had always to be counted as surprising faithfulness; it could never be presupposed. The future was uncertain.

The Davidic covenant presupposed the permanence of Yahweh's support of Israel through the perpetuation of the dynasty in Jerusalem. This emphasis on God's promised faithfulness encompassed forgiveness more easily but ran the risk of underestimating Yahweh's concern for justice and the lengths to which Yahweh would go to discipline the people.

Faced with the trauma of the exile which made both traditions appear bankrupt, Second Isaiah emphasized promised faithfulness without a king as mediator; the Priestly writer balanced the themes of promise and surprise in his paradigmatic treatment of God's response to Israel's sin in rejecting the land.

Yahweh's faithfulness to members of the covenant community was recognized in a variety of concrete expressions: in deliverance from enemies and oppressors, in ongoing protection, in bringing difficult circumstances to a turning point with long-range benefit. But most important, divine loyalty took shape in forgiveness, made known both in the restoration of personal communion and in the modifying of the concrete consequences of sin. In this respect especially was Yahweh's loyalty sure and abundant, far surpassing human loyalty which in ordinary usage of the word seems never to have been extended to forgiveness.

In the prophetic literature the concept of loyalty comes to have a special place in describing the response that Yahweh desires from Israel. With its connotation of concern for the weak or needy, loyalty undergirds the concepts of justice and righteousness by making clear that they are truly for all people, and most especially for those least likely to experience them. If Israel could truly live loyally, Yahweh's justice and righteousness would come alive in the community of faith. Furthermore, with its connotation of freely undertaken commitment, the prophetic view of Israel's loyalty challenges the notion of obedience based on fear and opens up the possibility that Israel's persistent failure of loyalty is deeply painful to God. In the face of the inability of the community to respond to divine pleading, the prophets look forward to a time of new covenant, when God will give the gift of loyal living to Israel and the community will truly know Yahweh.

In the meantime, God continues to honor whatever acts of loyalty frail mortals are able to perform. The corporate community and its members still hear the invitation to do justice, love loyalty, and walk humbly with God. Response takes shape in free sustaining of commitment to God and community, in individual acts of piety toward one's neighbors, and in concern for the upholding of justice. In a word, loyalty takes shape in willing and joyful observance of the Ten Commandments.

NEW TESTAMENT RESONANCES

Jonah's witness that God's loyalty extended even to forgiving the hated Ninevites opens the way for a new covenant in which forgiveness is proclaimed through Israel to all the world. The psalmist anticipated the theme in a different way in praising the loyalty of God made manifest in the very act of creating the world (Ps. 136:5–9). The Creator of all extends loyalty to all peoples of the world through Jesus of Nazareth, thus establishing in a new key the Abrahamic promise of blessing to the nations. The New Testament bears witness to Jesus as expression of God's continuing but transformed loyalty to the Davidic line. At the same time, it testifies to the ongoing role of Israel as a light to the nations, another way for the outpouring of divine loyalty in the world.[1]

## Abounding Loyalty

The prologue of John's Gospel expresses this testimony that God's loyalty is present in a new way in Jesus:

> And the Word became flesh and dwelt among us, full of grace and truth. (John 1:14)

The Greek behind the phrase "grace and truth" reflects the classic Hebrew combination "loyalty and faithfulness," or sure loyalty. It seems likely then that John's expression "full of" reflects correspondingly that other classic word "abundant" or "abounding," which was used in Israel's liturgy to describe the uniqueness of divine loyalty. In Christ, the world experiences in a unique way the abounding, sure loyalty of God. One might go on to suggest that the ministry of Jesus narrated in the Gospels confirms John's theological assessment. All the acts of Jesus' earthly life can be viewed as embodying what loyalty is really all about. Choose any pericope, and one finds Jesus portrayed as a person freely living out commitment to others, a person especially concerned for the downtrodden and outcast, those overlooked or ignored.

It is reasonable to ask why the Old Testament word we have translated "loyalty" should not simply be translated "grace," given this suggested background for John's words. The question calls to mind the great difficulty of translating the Hebrew term *ḥesed* itself, as was shown in chapter 1, "Introduction: Contemporary Experience and Ancient Witness." The translation "loyalty" has been used here to offer a consistent reference point and to invite a rethinking of the usability of the word to express aspects of biblical life style. The Hebrew word shifted somewhat in meaning in the course of the Old Testament period, and its meaning may have been understood yet differently by first century C.E. Jews and Christians. The situation is further complicated by the fact that, although grace (Greek *charis*) is usually recognized as the New Testament concept with the greatest affinity to Hebrew loyalty, the Greek Old Testament uses *charis* for a different Hebrew word (*ḥēn*, meaning "grace") and most frequently chooses *'eleos* ("mercy") for Hebrew "loyalty." Thus it is not surprising that "grace" or "mercy" rather than "loyalty" have often been suggested for translating *ḥesed*. Although there are many human situations where the words "grace" and "mercy" would seem unsuitable, in passages concentrating on God's forgiveness these terms would convey part of the picture. But commitment or obligation is a key nuance of the Hebrew word which we have noted over and over again; it seems to me that loyalty is able to suggest this nuance in a way grace and mercy do not. Short treatments of the New Testament concept of grace typically emphasize its connotation of an undeserved gift offered to those with whom God had no relationship (thus establishing a relationship). This interpretation sets aside that Hebrew nuance of commitment in the term "loyalty." It must be left to New Testament experts to say whether or in what way God's self-obligation is part of the New Testament concept of grace. My point is only that as Christians popularly understand the word "grace," it is inadequate in this respect to the fullness of the Old Testament concept of loyalty.

The apostle Paul's ringing assurance in Romans 8 that nothing in all creation can separate us from the love of God in Christ reflects the abounding sure loyalty of God. In the face of persecution and tribulation, peril and sword, Paul comes to know that God's loyalty goes even beyond deliverance from enemies, or constant protection, or bringing the situation right from a human point of view. For loyalty in the end even overcomes death—neither life nor death can separate us from the love of God. Thus God's loyalty is not to be measured by one's lot in life; it is promised despite all enemies. But to those who place their trust in God, it is promised as well despite all human failing and backsliding. So well did Paul argue the case for this sure promise that he had to warn against the false principle of continuing in sin that grace might abound (Rom. 6:1). Again the words suggest the Old Testament theme of abounding loyalty.

In the New Testament, as in the Old, promise and surprise needed to be held in tandem. If Paul emphasized promised loyalty, he surely recognized as well that God's enduring patience in the face of sin should ever remain a cause for amazement. But the situation of the early church was one of precarious existence against great odds, and in such a context promise to the faithful became appropriately the dominant note.

## Loyalty as New Testament Life Style

Any number of New Testament texts resonate with the themes of commitment freely lived out and special concern for the needy.[2] One might mention the Sermon on the Mount, or the definition of neighbor and responsibility illustrated in the parable of the Good Samaritan, or the plan for sharing of goods recorded in Acts 4, or the exhortation against partiality toward the well-dressed in James 2. Even the call to the rich to show liberality (1 Timothy 6) might be considered under the rubric of loyalty. In the face of such an impossible task, I simply select one compelling New Testament description of faithful life style which is congruent at its deepest level with the Old Testament perspective on loyalty as the appropriate life style for the community of faith. Paul writes:

> For you were called to freedom, [brothers and sisters]; only do not use your freedom as an opportunity for the flesh, but through love be servants of one another. For the whole law is fulfilled in one word, "You shall love your neighbor as yourself." . . .
> But I say, walk by the Spirit. . . . The fruit of the Spirit is love, joy, peace, patience, kindness, goodness, faithfulness, gentleness, self-control. (Gal. 5:13–14, 16a, 22–23a)

The choice of this passage could be debated, of course. Some might find the list of Spirit fruit too meek and thus hindering the "fight" for justice for the weak and those without an advocate. But only in such a Spirit can one challenge the enemy without hatred. Others might find the theme of service unacceptable for those already long in unwarranted servitude. But the call to loyal living is a call freely to use one's own strengths, whatever they may be, for serving others. And this the Galatians passage conveys. Freedom, service of the other, love of neighbor, and walking by the Spirit—in these are caught up the essence of biblical loyalty.

## CONTEMPORARY CONCERNS

In the light of this review of the biblical understanding of loyalty it seems reasonable to say that issues of loyalty are present implicitly if not explicitly in nearly every dimension of our daily lives. Insofar as we are relational beings, loyalty is always involved. Thus any discussion of contemporary concerns must be very selective and should be regarded as illustrative rather than exhaustive. Because the sampling of concerns must be very limited, readers are invited and urged to reflect upon which situations in their own lives raise questions of loyalty, and how this discussion might be helpful for those situations. In preparing this section, I have been especially helped by conversations with others, and I would lift up the value of communal reflection for any who pursue this topic.

*General Guidelines*

This volume opened with questions of divorce, a demand for dishonesty, gang warfare, and inconvenient needs of friends. What may the long intervening discussion of the biblical concept of loyalty offer as guidance to those who confront these problems, or to any of us in our own contexts of loyalty? How might a biblical life style modify or transform our usual approach to such issues of loyalty?

1. First of all, the Bible is clear that such a life style of loyalty depends in every way upon God's faithfulness. Divine faithfulness provides a model of loyalty which takes commitment radically seriously, which knows no fickleness, which gives attention both to the immediate neighbor and to the far-flung horizon of all humanity. In experiencing God's faithfulness, we find strength to keep trying to live loyally in the midst of human confusion and uncertainty, in the midst of opposition, in the midst of dejection and frustration. The faithful God overcomes our failure of loyalty and in forgiveness sets our feet again and again on the right path. The God who does justice, loyalty, and righteousness (Jer. 9:24) is the ground and source and perfecter and judge of all human loyalty.

2. In the second place, it is clear from our discussion of the biblical material that there are no easy answers for difficult situations, and that there is no single correct answer that can be applied to all similar cases. Loyalty as the Bible uses the word cannot be reduced to absolutes, such as never join a gang, never lie, always

support your company, never divorce, always help out when called upon.

In the absence of absolute rules, the demands of differing relationships often put claims of loyalty into competition and even conflict. The biblical narratives are full of persons making very hard and ambiguous choices; Sarah, Hushai, Rahab, Ruth—their choices seem obvious only in retrospect. In the moment of decision many choices are for one good over another. So a decision about whether to place a relative in a nursing home involves consideration of what needs will be met or not met for other family members as well. A decision about whether to dismiss (or to promote) an employee has ramifications for co-workers as well as for the individual and any economic dependents. Because complexity makes decisions more difficult, we tend to view loyalty in too narrow a framework in order to reach a decision and then to justify it to ourselves as the only possible decision. The biblical view of loyalty can open us to the complexity of the network of human interconnections, and it can free us to admit that our perspectives are limited and our choices are relative.

Even loyalty that is essentially focused on only one person can require difficult choices. If a child commits a misdemeanor, do parents show loyalty to that child by covering up what has happened or by reporting the child to the authorities? Should the spouse of an alcoholic cover for the drinker to protect job or social standing, or should the alcoholic be exposed as a means to move toward rehabilitation? No single answer is always the best. What the needy person asks for is not always the loyal thing to do; whether the choice is right is not possible to know for certain in advance.

3. In the third place, a strategy for loyal help which finally does not work for good need not automatically be regarded as an act of disloyalty, biblically speaking. At issue, rather, is how the decision was made, how the strategy was arrived at. If Hushai had been discovered in his infiltration plot, his attempt still would have been counted as loyalty to David. If a person makes every effort to support a friend, for the sake of the friend, and yet is rebuffed, loyalty has still been carried through.

On the other hand, a beneficial outcome is in itself no proof of loyal action toward the other. Naturally a beneficial outcome is desirable from the standpoint of the needy, however it is achieved. But living loyally before God involves considering the world from God's viewpoint and making choices for the sake of others rather than oneself. Apart from such a perspective, action is self-centered, not loyal, regardless of the outcome; only such a perspective offers a check and critique of our self-centeredness. If a child's crime is covered up only to preserve the parent's social status, or if the crime is revealed in a fit of anger which seeks revenge, then loyalty has not been operative regardless of the long-range outcome for the child's behavior and future. If a legislator supports a good cause only to ensure reelection, not out of any concern for the people whom the cause was intended to serve, then loyalty has not been operative. Action may be counted biblically as loyalty only insofar as it is based in loyal intent. At best, such action incorporates also some effort to communicate the loyal intent of the decision.

4. This is not to say, of course, that any decision is acceptable so long as one's heart is in the right place. Ahab was judged wrong by God for his "loyal" deal with Ben-hadad. Israel's "loyal" litany of repentance in Hosea's time was inadequate to the situation. So, in the fourth place, the standard of evaluation lies ultimately in some right understanding of what God is about in the world and of how one's own acts of loyalty, big or small, are congruent with that understanding. In any effort to assess the options for loyal action, it seems to me that communal conversation and reflection are absolutely critical. We all stand in need of the corrective and the enlarged horizons which can come from dialogue about the character of God's loyal intention for the world and also about which strategies for our own loyalty are most congruent with God's intention and may best embody it.

H. Richard Niebuhr has described God's intention and the appropriate human response under the rubric of "radical monotheism." Niebuhr views loyalty or faithfulness as the "active" side of the faith relation, paired with trust as the "passive" side. He argues that the goal appropriate to radical monotheism is to live a moral life based on a commitment to all others as neighbor, "as companion in being," just as God manifests loyalty to all creation, not just to a particular subgroup. To live in such a way requires one to stand against the pressure in culture and even in religion itself toward "henotheistic" living in which the neighbor is functionally limited to members of one's own group, however that group is defined.[3]

I find Niebuhr's work helpful in placing the vision of the reign of God in the widest possible perspective. It holds the hope and goal of a *shalom* community before me in a way which affirms that God showed loyalty to Nineveh and that I am called to do no less. All who desire to live loyally must keep on wrestling to know what is important in the world, what life ought to be, and how they may join with others toward embodying God's loyalty to the world. Israel's history, and indeed the history of the church, shows a long record of being too sure too soon about what God was doing and what was expected of the faithful. If we trust that God's will is ultimately for a *shalom* community, then we should be ever open to the possibility of an unimagined "new thing" happening (Isa. 43:18–19; Jer. 31:22) and be ready to live in such a way as to allow the new to spring forth. At the same time, we must not let uncertainty about the right course of action lead us into total paralysis. Now we know only in part, so loyalty also requires taking the risk of missing God's way, while trusting that God will use others in the community to correct our unwitting mistakes.

5. The many-faceted biblical testimony to God's loyalty to all creation (Genesis, Jonah, Second Isaiah, John, Romans) to which Niebuhr gives one form of theological expression does not translate into the unchangeability of all personal and institutional relationships into which we happen to enter. Rather, all relationships should be assessed in terms of what God is doing and how we may best at any given time embody God's loyalty. In the fifth place, therefore, biblical loyalty does not require that every relationship be continued indefinitely in an unchanging form. Ruth, for example, showed great loyalty in accompanying Naomi, but Orpah did not show disloyalty by returning home. There is room for a person to change jobs, even though the first employer makes a strong plea

for the essential role of that individual. A decision to move on
need not be the occasion for a guilt trip. By the same token, loyalty
does leave room for an employee to be let go, although it is
extraordinarily difficult to avoid an experience of bitterness and
betrayal. The biblical tradition apparently handled such concluding of relationships by committing the needy to God's care. Perhaps such explicitly religious language would seem a cop-out today, but institutions need to find concrete ways of easing departure
pain. Innovations in the areas of counseling, retraining, relocating,
severance pay, and the like are steps in the direction of loyalty.
Other relationships may also be ended, and the closure may, even
in itself, be an act of loyalty. It is conceivable that allowing a
friendship to drift into limbo, to "lose track" of another, can
partake of loyalty (although all too often such drifting reflects our
own need rather than any assessment of the condition of the
other). We must accept our finitude and work within it: any one
person can sustain only a limited number of relationships at a given
time. Where there is lessening need, it may be loyal to others to let
some friendships lie fallow.

In my own view (although, of course, some would debate it),
even the ending of a marriage may in some instances be a loyal
rather than a disloyal act of the two persons *toward each other.*
Marriages do not always grow toward maturity. If mutual support
is outweighed by mutual destructiveness, and if personal characteristics and social circumstances preclude any real possibility for
change, then loyalty may call for concluding the relationship.

Illustrations could be multiplied. Changing of citizenship, giving
up of ethnic or racial ties, changing one's church membership to a
different local congregation within the same community—none of
these actions is inherently disloyal.

6. On the other hand, a life style informed by biblical loyalty
will never take any relationship lightly or let it come to an end
without serious reflection. It is extraordinarily difficult to sort out
our reasoning so that we can distinguish our own convenience or
pleasure from what is really in the best interest of the other(s).
Rationalizing a decision is all too easy. Consequently, in the sixth
place, everything that has been said of marriages, friendships,

employment, or other relationships in the preceding section must be viewed from the opposite perspective as well. Relationships almost by definition require work to be maintained; to abandon them at the first bump in the road, or even in the midst of a long rocky stretch, may be to fail in loyalty. The assessment of incompatibility should be made by difficult standards, not casual ones.

On a global level the debate over "triage" in facing the question of world hunger illustrates the difficulty of loyal decision making about the limits of human relationship. Should some people be deliberately "written off" to starvation so that other groups in less dire straits may be assured of survival? Or does loyalty require that we attempt to feed everyone, trusting that the effort itself will finally "bear fruit" in some change of global politics and economics that will put food on every table? Is God's loyalty embodied better by keeping more people alive or by trying to share without categorizing? People of deep moral conviction have argued on both sides of this issue.

In sum, loyalty by definition requires steadfastness in relationship. The challenge lies in discovering how to embody that steadfastness in faithful action which is informed by God's concern for the world rather than by deluded self-interest. Any human manifestation of loyalty is bound to be proximate—because our motives are so rarely pure, because most choices for showing loyalty involve ancillary consequences we might not desire, because our human nature is such that our best steadfastness turns out to be more fragile than we like to admit. Nonetheless, our weakness and uncertainty need not paralyze us. We make our choices for faithful living recognizing that not every wrong choice is disloyal and realizing that not every relationship can or should be arbitrarily continued. Above all, we make our choices trusting in God's great loyalty—loyalty that forgives our misunderstandings of the *shalom* vision, loyalty that forgives our lack of steadfastness in embodying even what we do know aright, and loyalty that in the end despite all odds will bring the world round right.

Questions of loyalty are particularly pressing today in four institutions of our society—family, employment, nation-state, and church—in North America in particular but in other parts of the world as well. What concerns might be raised from a biblical perspective? Each of these topics has been anticipated in the illustrations of the general guidelines. Again I would urge readers to name the arenas most important to them, and to identify their own questions and concerns for those arenas as well as for the four discussed in the following paragraphs.

*Family*

The marriage vow is one of the few public statements of commitment that our society recognizes in the sphere of primary interpersonal relationships. Contemporary uncertainty and dis-ease about long-term commitments show themselves in many ways in the context of the decision to marry: the transformation of vows into legal contracts that lay out all rights and duties in advance; the advice to a soon-to-be-married young woman, "Don't worry, you can always get divorced"; "trial" living together, in which each becomes afraid either to ask for or to offer commitment; marriages with specified ending dates subject to renewal. Ironically enough, many such signs of the fragility of loyalty probably are attempts to generate loyalty. To the extent that they indicate a desire for responsible commitment, they may be a hopeful sign. Yet most of these alternatives rule out by definition the possibility of faithfulness no matter what. God's faithfulness in all circumstances suggests that our own commitments should not seek to know every contingency in advance.

Unlike the husband-wife relationship, the relationship between parents and children is not one that is stated publicly in any formal way. The expectations are not so self-evident. Recently many families have become more self-conscious about their decision to have or not to have children. The possibility for relating loyally to one's child may be enhanced by the recognition that having a child means an irrevocable commitment. (Even giving an infant up for adoption does not anymore necessarily end that commitment forever.) But such careful family planning may backfire in unreasonable expectations placed upon a child who becomes merely an instrument for a parent's self-gratification.

Questions of loyalty surface in choices between children and career, however they are adjudicated in single-parent or traditional or extended family living. Each person must consider the best way to use his or her God-given gifts for the whole world. But choices do preclude other choices, and sometimes permanently so. Not all careers can be resumed after several or many years' hiatus.

Children likewise lack guidelines in relating to parents. From teen-age peer pressure in conflict with family values, to independence in career choice, to retired adults facing the changing needs of their ninety-year-old parents, the challenge of being loyal to one's parents and true to oneself faces people of all ages.

Even less defined are the expectations for relationships within various kinds of nontraditional family units. Too often these alternative families are either ignored or treated as aberrations which should be converted as much as possible into conventional marriage-and-children patterns. Their persistence, viability, typicality in other cultures, etc., are quite overlooked. Perhaps loyalty calls the traditionalists instead to join with people in nontraditional families for mutual learning about varieties of committed life styles.

## Institution/Vocation

Corporations and other employing institutions place many written and unwritten demands upon their employees. While these might not be labeled "loyalty tests," they often function as such. Teachers in public schools may be expected to hold particular views of their subject matter. Researchers may be pressured to "fudge" data, stock analysts to forget inconvenient facts. Many institutions, especially religious ones, consider the employee as "their own" even when not "on duty," so that personal life style becomes a criterion for continued employment even when it does not impinge upon effectiveness on the job. Business executives may be expected to live in a certain geographic area or to belong to certain clubs or to entertain in a particular style. Employers of all kinds are prone to become uneasy with employees who disagree, who ask too many questions, who would like to do things differently.

I have already suggested that loyalty allows for changing jobs and for letting employees go. But the choices are not simple for the employee whose own vision of *shalom* is violated by an employer's expectations. No employer, present or future, may fully satisfy the vision of *shalom* held by the employee; a job change may have economic consequences for dependents; the possibilities of eventual change of the employing institution from within must be weighed against the present moral compromise. However such questions are resolved, biblical living here as in the family means loyalty first to God. Loyalty to an employer is not automatic or an area bracketed off from one's embodiment of the good news of God's care. To use a traditional expression, a Christian in any walk of life should be considered to be in "full-time Christian service."

Since in our society most employees are inevitably dependent upon their employers for economic survival, it should fall particularly to employers as the ones who wield power in this context to give careful consideration to their expectations of employees. An institution should ask itself seriously what relevance its personal expectations have to performance, and whether its performance expectations are commensurate with community wholeness in the fullest sense. In any but the smallest companies, such questions may seem impossible to address, because the power center is so difficult to locate. Yet some individuals do have limited power to exercise loyalty toward those who have even less control in such bureaucratic networks. Each is called to weigh the risks and opportunities of the choices available. And in this arena especially, sharing of stories may help individuals and even institutions to discover fresh and freeing choices that have simply gone unnoticed.

*Patriotism*

What does it mean to be a loyal American, or a loyal citizen of any nation-state? Niebuhr observes that when a modern nation seeks to govern by consent rather than by power alone, it justifies its existence and invites citizen loyalty by pledging the state to some cause beyond itself (such as "liberty and justice for all") to which the citizens can commit themselves.[4] The question for those seeking to embody a *shalom* vision is threefold: First, is the state's cause (or more often, causes) congruent with a biblical world view which lifts up God's concern for all people, especially the weak? Second, are the strategies of the state (its economic, military, diplomatic policies, etc.) congruent with the causes espoused? Third, if the causes or strategies should be changed, what means of influencing governmental policies are appropriate to loyal living?

Although Old Testament Israel was much more analogous to the church than to a modern secular nation-state, its people did have to face similar questions. For even then the cause of the nation got split away from the will of God, as the poor were forgotten in the press of economic expansion or as military buildup was carried to unnecessary lengths. In those times the prophets gave correction to the people's misunderstanding of what their loyalty should really look like. But in those times there were frequently competing (and often sincere) prophets with differing perspectives on God's will (cf. the story of Hananiah in Jeremiah 27—28). The choices were no easier in the time of making them. Only in retrospect did the Jewish community identify the "true" prophets and preserve their writings in the canon.

So we also must struggle with choices in the midst of our own situation. What should be the response of one who disagrees with the government's budget priorities? Should the challenge be made only through the ballot box and lobbying, or should it extend to the refusal to pay taxes? Here, as everywhere, it is difficult to distinguish rationale from rationalization. Not paying taxes might be simply to avoid the bother of paperwork or to have more money for oneself; paying the taxes might be simply from fear of the legal consequences of such civil disobedience. How should refusal to register for a potential draft be balanced against the long-range consequences of losing government subsidy for education for a humanity-serving profession? Such strategic questions could be multiplied; the questions about the mission (cause) of one's country are equally difficult. To what extent, for example, is it the obligation of America to encourage democracy elsewhere? (And what strategies are appropriate—food? arms? advisers?) Whatever the question, to live loyally before God, to seek to embody God's loyalty as biblically understood, means that the state cannot be simply equated with God's way. The state may be a means toward *shalom*, but a limited and penultimate means.

At the same time, there should be room for some old-fashioned (or perhaps new-fashioned) patriotism. We should seek ways to support and celebrate whatever the state does that furthers God's kind of loyalty. Loyalty to the state as to any human institution must be selective, partial, and subsumed under rather than equated with loyalty to God.

## The Church

One might suppose that the church would be a stronghold for faithfulness in action, but as a human institution it too can experience failure of loyalty. Again the story of Israel is pertinent, as the people repeatedly lost sight of God's intention for their own community, an intention that had implications for the world as well. The New Testament shows us that the early church was full of disputes about the intention of God for the world (e.g., the admission of Gentiles, Acts 15) and about proper life style within the church family (e.g., eating of food sacrificed to idols, the place of women in worship, disciplining of backsliders). So also today, Christians are scarcely of one mind about God's intention for the world or about the role of the church in the world.

How might a local congregation model loyalty within its own membership and to the community in such an environment? One significant role of the church may be to help its own members explore the dynamics of decision making in the various arenas, such as family, vocation, and nation, where issues of loyalty are at stake. The exploration would be carried out in such a way that people come to see the complexity of choices and something of the theological underpinnings of the alternative positions. Whether nuclear disarmament, the death penalty, meatless meals, homosexuality, or corporal punishment of small children, no issue is too big or too small to be viewed from the perspective of faithfulness in action. But most important, having helped people to think through an issue, the congregation might seek for ways to support and honor the differing conclusions reached by its members. Loyalty takes shape in continuation of dialogue and in serving the other despite disagreement. Humility befits all who seek to discover God's will. When the dialogue results in consequences for congregational policy, such as building use or budget allocation, those who support the final decision might show loyalty by cultivating common perspectives on other issues with the dissenters; those who question the decision might show loyalty by continuing the discussion from within. The prophets of Israel regularly identified themselves with their people, however misguided the people were, and we know that Jeremiah sometimes agonized over whether his message was true. The possibility of leaving a congregation has already been mentioned as an option. If such should come to pass as loyalty, it would surely take place in the context of pain and dialogue, not bad-mouthing and backbiting.

A seeking congregation may find many ways to express loyalty toward those in need in its own community or far away. The challenge here will be to remain steadfast in such commitments even when the recipients prove "unworthy" from a human point of view: to send another shipment of food even when the recipients do not say thank you; to keep the church open even when the drop-in group vandalizes the social hall. In such steadfastness the congregation may embody for others as well as for itself the steadfastness of God's faithfulness to all people.

LOYALTY AND LIBERATION

Because biblical loyalty involves steadfast commitment to others embodied in action to support their needs, it is a conception that addresses everyone at some level; part of being human is to be involved in relationships. The biblical conception of loyalty as living the Decalogue, love of God and neighbor, provides a frame of reference from which people can begin to assess the choices available to them from the point of view of God's loyalty to all humanity.

But although a loyal life style is for everyone, the conception should speak with special force to any who find themselves in a position of power or privilege vis-à-vis others in the world. For it is under the rubric of loyalty that the Bible draws special attention to the need of the poor, downtrodden, outcast, silenced, powerless, or simply overlooked. It is loyalty's steadfast commitment to the weak that will enable justice to prevail for all people. It is loyalty which will ensure that no one is forgotten in building the *shalom* community. It is through loyalty that the vision of God's reign is kept colorful and diverse, not monochromatic and homogeneous.

The biblical conception of loyalty thus resonates with the concern of liberation theology to describe the place of people such as white, prosperous North Americans in the struggle of the oppressed. The dangers of the handout, of do-good condescension, of deciding what the oppressed need, are all too evident. But I would suggest that loyalty, biblically understood, may provide a helpful image for the powerful.[5] Loyalty would imply solidarity, not identification; it would mean letting the oppressed define their own need; it would mean not taking pride in "band-aid" solutions to systemic problems; it would mean a "theology of relinquishment"[6]—relinquishment of power, privilege, economic advantage. Loyalty as free commitment would mean joining hands not because of guilt feelings but out of a common hope that the creation itself will one day be set free (Rom. 8:21).

A FINAL REMINDER

The preceding pages have had a great deal to say about our embodiment of God's loyalty to the world in a personal and communal life style of faithfulness in action. But such a life style does not, indeed cannot, emerge in and of itself. The biblical witness is very clear that loyalty can exist, however frail it is, only as response to the communal and personal experience of God's faithfulness to us. It is God's loyalty that motivates our loyalty, that strengthens our loyalty when it falters, that corrects our loyalty when it is misplaced, that helps us to hold fast to the *shalom* vision and to boast aright:

> Let not the wise boast in wisdom,
> let not the strong boast in strength,

let not the rich boast in riches,
    but let the one who boasts boast in this:
in understanding and knowing that I am Yahweh,
    Doer of loyalty and justice and righteousness in the earth.
                    (Jer. 9:23–24, au. trans. and versification)

Only after we know that Yahweh is "Doer of loyalty and justice and righteousness in the earth" can we heed the ancient words of Micah:

And what does Yahweh ask of you
    but to do justice, and to love loyalty,
    and to walk attentively with your God?
                    (Mic. 6:8, au. trans.)


## NOTES

1. In the providence of God the Jewish community still continues in this role, despite the long, tragic history of efforts to snuff it out. To be sure, this ongoing role of Israel is given but muted expression in the New Testament by comparison to its emphasis on the new way of Jesus of Nazareth. Already the writings of the earliest church reflect the competition and rivalry between Jews and Christians as two groups "regarding each other as apostates from the truth and wanderers from the Way of the One God of whom they both claimed to be beloved." (Paul M. van Buren, *Discerning the Way: A Theology of the Jewish Christian Reality* [New York: Seabury Press, 1980], 61.) The Christian teaching of the displacement of the Jews emerged early and has been called into serious theological question only in the last part of the present century. See van Buren, esp. 60–67, 132–38, 197–201, for a sensitive Christian exploration of the relationship between Judaism and Christianity.

2. The theme of the undergirding of communal justice at the level of a judicial system is less significant, since the New Testament church had no political power or authority.

3. H. Richard Niebuhr, *Radical Monotheism and Western Culture* (New York: Harper & Brothers, 1960), esp. 16–23, 32–35. Niebuhr prefers the phrase "principle of being" and avoids the use of the term "God" in describing his concept of radical monotheism, perhaps because of his painful observations about the ways in which the religions of Christianity and Judaism have domesticated God and thus have slid into various forms of henotheism.

4. Niebuhr, *Radical Monotheism*, 65–68.

5. Bruce Birch and Larry Rasmussen have discussed the dilemma of the

prosperous and have suggested a number of such biblical images in their *Predicament of the Prosperous* (Philadelphia: Westminster Press, 1978). This approach to loyalty is offered as a supplement to their very helpful reflections.

6. See Marie Augusta Neal, *A Socio-Theology of Letting Go: The Role of a First World Church Facing Third World Peoples* (New York: Paulist Press, 1977), 103–11.

# Scripture Index

Verse numbers follow the English text. Boldfaced page numbers
indicate extended discussion of the passage.

OLD TESTAMENT

| Genesis | | Exodus | |
|---|---|---|---|
| 1—50 | 140 | 19—24 | **42–46** |
| 12 | 27, 37 nn. 19–20, | 19:8 | 45 |
| | 79 n.25 | 20—23 | 45 |
| 17 | 75 | 20 | 43 |
| 17:13 | 66 | 20:3 | 44 |
| 20 | **26–28,** 37 nn. | 20:5b–6 | 43 |
| | 19–20 | 20:22— | |
| 20:5 | 27 | 23:33 | 43 |
| 20:13 | 27 | 21:22 | 130 n.30 |
| 21 | 41 | 22:26–27 | 102 |
| 21:22–34 | 76 | 24 | 47 |
| 21:23 | 29 | 24:3 | 45 |
| 23 | 37 n.22 | 32—34 | **47–51,** |
| 24 | 30, 31 | | 78 n.18 |
| 24:8 | 31 | 32:10 | 48 |
| 24:12–14 | 91 | 32:11–12 | 73 |
| 24:27 | 91 | 33 | 58, 95, 123 |
| 24:41 | 31 | 33:12–17 | 40 |
| 24:49 | 31 | 33:16 | 48 |
| 26 | 37 n.19 | 34 | 71, 74 |
| 32 | 86 | 34:6–7 | 73, 98 n.3 |
| 32:10–11 | 86 | 34:6b–7 | 47 |
| 35 | 37 n.22 | | |
| 39:21 | 90 | | |
| 47 | 28 | Leviticus | |
| 50 | 28 | 19:2 | 3 |

| | | | |
|---|---|---|---|
| 6:1–6 | **104–7** | *Joel* | |
| 6:1–3 | 106 | 2:13 | 49–50 |
| 6:3 | 109 | | |
| 6:4–6 | 105–6 | *Amos* | |
| 6:4 | 114, 118 | 1:11 | 35 n.4 |
| 6:6 | 106, 107, 108, | 3:2 | 52 |
| | 111, 122 | 5:25 | 129 n.20 |
| 6:9 | 120 | 9:7–10 | 50 |
| 7:6–10 | 120 | | |
| 7:13b | 117 | *Jonah* | |
| 8:2 | 109 | 1—4 | 50–51, 140 |
| 8:4 | 80 n.36 | | |
| 8:11 | 110 | *Micah* | |
| 8:12 | 117 | 6 | 115, 118, 120, 127 |
| 10:1 | 110 | 6:1–5 | 127 n.1 |
| 10:12–13a | 119 | 6:2 | 103 |
| 10:12 | 119, 122 | 6:6–8 | **101–4,** |
| 10:13 | 119, 121 | | 127 n.1 |
| 10:13b | 120 | 6:6 | 101 |
| 11:1–2a | 117 | 6:7 | 102 |
| 11:5 | 117 | 6:8 | 3, 101, 106, |
| 11:8 | 121 | | 118, 127, |
| 11:8a | 117 | | 127 n.3, |
| 11:8c | 117 | | 128 n.7, |
| 11:9 | 4, 121, 123 | | 128 n.12, 150 |
| 12 | 119, 120 | 7:1–7 | 124–25 |
| 12:4c | 118 | 7:2 | 124 |
| 12:6 | 118, 119, 122 | 7:3 | 124 |
| 12:7 | 119 | 7:5–6 | 124 |
| 13:1–2 | 120 | 7:7 | 124 |
| 13:5–6 | 110 | 7:18–20 | 70–71 |
| 13:9 | 121 | 7:20 | 128 n.18 |

## New Testament

| | | | |
|---|---|---|---|
| *Luke* | | 8 | 135 |
| 14:12–14 | 128 n.5 | 8:21 | 149 |
| *John* | | *Galatians* | |
| 1—21 | 140 | 5:13–23a | 136 |
| 1:14 | 134 | *1 Timothy* | |
| *Acts* | | 6 | 136 |
| 4 | 136 | | |
| 15 | 147 | *Hebrews* | |
| | | 11 | 23 |
| *Romans* | | *James* | |
| 1—16 | 140 | 2 | 136 |
| 6:1 | 135 | | |